Academic Writing Skills

Teacher's Manual

1

Peter Chin   Samuel Reid

Sean Wray   Yoko Yamazaki

CAMBRIDGE
UNIVERSITY PRESS

CAMBRIDGE
UNIVERSITY PRESS

University Printing House, Cambridge CB2 8BS, United Kingdom

One Liberty Plaza, 20th Floor, New York, NY 10006, USA

477 Williamstown Road, Port Melbourne, VIC 3207, Australia

314-321, 3rd Floor, Plot 3, Splendor Forum, Jasola District Centre, New Delhi - 110025, India

79 Anson Road, #06-04/06, Singapore 079906

Cambridge University Press is part of the University of Cambridge.

It furthers the University's mission by disseminating knowledge in the pursuit of education, learning and research at the highest international levels of excellence.

www.cambridge.org
Information on this title: www.cambridge.org/9781107642935

© Cambridge University Press 2012

First published 2012
Reprinted 2018

A catalogue record for this publication is available from the British Library

ISBN 978-1-107-64293-5 paperback Teacher's Manual 1
ISBN 978-1-107-63622-4 paperback Student's Book 1

Contributors: Peter Chin, Samuel Reid, Sean Wray, Yoko Yamazaki
Editor: Sean Wray

Academic Writing Skills has been developed by the Research and Development team at Waseda University International Co., Ltd., Tokyo.

Contents

Introduction to the Teacher's Manual

Academic Writing Skills is a three-level series which introduces the essential skills and strategies required to compose academic essays. *Academic Writing Skills 1* is the first book in the series. It contains four units, with each divided into parts (12 parts total in the book). An appendix of writing points is attached at the end of the book.

The *Academic Writing Skills 1 Teacher's Manual* has two parts:

Part 1: Lesson plans for each part of each unit (12 lesson plans total)

Part 2: The answer key to the exercises

General tips on using the textbook in class

For teachers and students, the textbook is designed to be followed directly. Therefore, each part of each unit has the following features:

1. **The goals of the lesson,** listed in bullet points at the beginning.
2. **Sections introducing teaching points** which describe a particular aspect of academic writing.
3. **Examples and exercises** to help deepen students' understanding of the teaching points.
4. **Review questions,** listed at the end to review the teaching points.

To best utilize the book's features and class time, it is suggested that teachers:

1. **State lesson goals.**
    Lesson goals are listed at the beginning of each part in the textbook. State these goals and/or write them on the board at the beginning of the lesson so students are focused on what they should be learning.
2. **Avoid lengthy explanations.**
    *   Elicit key words and concepts from the students whenever possible. Students may have read the points (if assigned as homework) or may already have some knowledge of these points.
    *   Use concept check questions to make sure students understand both the components of an essay and their purpose.
3. **Have students work in pairs or groups.**
    Students can support each other's learning by doing the exercises or checking their answers collaboratively. A suggested size for small groups is 3 or 4 students.
4. **Review the lesson points.**
    Use the Review Questions (listed at the end of each part) at the end of the class or at the beginning of the next class to check students' understanding.

Assigning homework

1. **Reading** Reading of particular teaching points from the textbook can be assigned as homework. This will help when teaching these points in class, as students when elicited will be better able to answer questions on the points.

2. **Writing** The textbook presents individual aspects of essay writing, but does not contain a specific essay writing task. It is recommended that an essay writing task be assigned to supplement the lessons. Students can apply what they learn in each lesson to this writing task so that by a certain point in the course, they will have a completed academic essay.

The textbook uses academic topics, so the assigned essay should ideally be on an academic topic that can be answered in a five-paragraph essay. Sample academic topics are:

- *The internet and its effect on education in your home country*
- *Is foreign language education in kindergarten too early for children?*
- *Gender equality rankings are consistently high in Scandinavian countries. Explain some of the major reasons for this.*
- *Some say developed countries should increase financial aid to poor countries. Others say developed countries should reduce such aid. Argue for one of the sides on this issue.*

Lesson plans

How to use the lesson plans

The lesson plans in this teacher's manual supplement the textbook by offering suggestions for:

- presenting the teaching points (the explanation under each section heading)
- conducting the practice exercises

There are a number of suggestions for each section. However, these suggestions are not meant to be followed in order. Rather, they should be viewed as a menu to choose from. Teachers should feel free to use some, all, or none of these ideas, or alternatively to supplement the textbook with their own ideas.

Text in the lesson plans that appears in *italics* denotes a suggested question or useful information to ask or share with students. Answers to the suggested questions appear in **bold** and follow (Answer) or (Possible answer).

Introducing academic essays

Before starting on Unit 1, Part 1, it may be useful to present what an academic essay is. A possible procedure is:

1. In pairs or small groups, have students discuss: *What makes an essay "academic"?*
2. Elicit answers.
3. Have students read textbook pages v–vi, "Introduction to academic writing."
4. Books closed. In pairs or small groups, have students summarize to each other what they just read.
5. Check understanding by asking questions on the contents of pages v – vi:
   - *What are five aspects of academic writing?*
   - *What are some possible purposes of writing an academic essay?*
   - *What are some points to keep in mind about the audience?*
   - *etc.*

UNIT 1

Part 1
Getting ready to write

Section 1 — What is a paragraph?

Option 1

1. Introduce the idea of a paragraph by having students discuss these questions with a partner:
   - *What is a paragraph?*
   - *What information should a paragraph include?*
2. Then have students read the explanation in the textbook.

Option 2

1. Have students read the information.
2. Check students' understanding by asking:
   - *How many topics should a paragraph contain?* (Answer: **1**)
   - *What should every sentence in the paragraph describe?* (Answer: **The topic of the paragraph**)
3. Emphasize:
   - *The purpose of a paragraph is to explain one idea.*

Exercise 1

Option 1

1. After reading the paragraph on page 3, give students a few minutes to think about the answers to these questions individually.
2. Then have students discuss these questions in pairs or small groups.

Option 2

1. After reading the paragraph on page 3, have students close their books and, in pairs or small groups, summarize what the paragraph was about to each other.
2. Then have students discuss question 2.

Section 2 — The structure of a paragraph

Option 1

1. Regarding the paragraph structure, elicit from students:
   - *What are the three parts of a paragraph?*
   - *What is the purpose of each part?*
2. Write them on the board.

Option 2

1. Have students read the explanation of the three components of a paragraph (page 4).

2. Have students close their textbook and summarize what they read to a partner.
3. Ask the questions from Option 1.

Option 3

1. Draw a diagram of a paragraph on the board. Use lines to represent sentences instead of actual words.
2. Number the first line "1," the middle lines "2," and the final line "3."

   Have students match a number to the three terms, e.g.:

   ① _____

   ② _____

   _____

   _____

   _____

   _____

   ③ _____

Exercise 2

Option 1

1. Have students do parts 1 and 2 individually.
2. In pairs or small groups, have students compare answers.

Option 2

1. Follow Option 1 above.
2. Then have students:
   - underline the controlling idea in the topic sentence.
   - circle the concluding sentence.
   - write a number next to each supporting point.

Option 3

1. After Option 1 or 2, elicit from students:
   - *How many sentences explain each supporting point?*
   OR
   - *How might this paragraph (on page 3) be different from other paragraphs you have written?*

   (Possible answer: **It is much longer than the three- or four-sentence paragraphs often taught prior to university.**)

2. Emphasize:
   - *Academic paragraphs often reach eight or nine sentences or longer. This is necessary to properly support the controlling idea.*
   - *Because academic paragraphs are often of this longer length, a concluding sentence is often necessary to summarize the supporting points and reaffirm how they support the controlling idea or thesis.*

Section 3 — Generating ideas for writing – brainstorming

Option 1

Prior to explaining the three brainstorming methods:

1. Have students read the introductory information.

2. Have students, in pairs or small groups, quickly discuss any of the following questions:
   - *Have you ever used brainstorming techniques before? If so when and for what purpose?*
   - *In what situations do people brainstorm for ideas?*
   - *What are the different ways to brainstorm for ideas?*

3. Elicit answers.

Option 2

After presenting "listing":

1. Have students, in pairs or small groups, come up with a list for item 1 in Exercise 3 (page 7): "Reasons for studying abroad."

2. Tell students they have two minutes to complete this task. Keep time.

3. Elicit answers and compile them on the board into one long list.

Option 3

After presenting "listing":

1. Have students, in pairs or small groups, try to add more ideas to the list on page 5.

2. Then have students try to put the ideas into categories, e.g.:
   - "to get a good job ...," "to think about the future" = career

Option 4

After presenting "mind mapping":

1. Have students, in pairs or small groups, come up with a mind map for item 2 in Exercise 3 (page 7): "Advantages of joining a university organization."

2. Tell students they have two minutes to complete this task. Keep time.

3. Elicit answers and compile them on the board into one giant mind map.

Option 5

After presenting "mind mapping":

1. Have students, in pairs or small groups, add more ideas to the mind map on page 6.

2. Then have students discuss:
   - *Which ideas would you use if you had to write an essay on this topic?*

Option 6

After presenting "free writing":

1. Have students individually free write sentences on item 3 in Exercise 3: "Causes of stress among university students."

2. Tell students they have three minutes to complete this task. Keep time.

3. When time is up, in pairs or small groups, have students swap and read each other's free writing.

4. Emphasize:
   - *"Free writing" is not only useful when brainstorming, but also when writing the first draft of an essay. Often at the beginning of the writing process, students spend too much time thinking and not enough time writing. Free writing is a way to avoid over-thinking what to write and wasting time.*

Option 7

If students had a chance to practice all three of the methods:

1. Have them discuss in small groups:
   - *What are the advantages/disadvantages of each brainstorming style?*

   AND/OR
   - *Which brainstorming method was easiest for you and why?*

2. Elicit answers.

Option 8

Explain the following additional points regarding brainstorming:

1. *Brainstorming can be done alone but will be better if more people are involved.*

2. *Students often hesitate to write ideas they feel may not be appropriate. However, brainstorming should be a quick activity where the objective is quantity, not quality, of ideas.*

3. *Although many ideas may be generated when brainstorming, writers will need to be selective in which ideas to write about. Some ideas are more important than others, so it is up to individual writers to determine what the most important ideas are.*

Exercise 3

Option 1

1. Have students do the exercise individually.

2. In pairs or small groups, have students compare answers.

3. Poll students to see who prefers a particular method. Elicit reasons why.

Option 2

1. Have students work in pairs or small groups to brainstorm ideas.

2. Have one person in each pair or group write down the ideas.

3. After two or three minutes, have each pair/group circle the ideas that they think are the most useful.

4. Elicit answers from the writers.

Option 3

1. Follow Option 2 above.

2. Then have each pair/group exchange their brainstorm with another pair/group.

3. Have students add additional ideas to the new brainstorm they get from the other pair/group.

Option 4

1. Make this activity into a race between different groups:
   - Set a target number of ideas that need to be reached – the first group to reach this number of ideas is the winner.

2. Emphasize:
   - *Brainstorming is about quantity rather than quality.*

Section 4 Writing a topic sentence

Option 1

1. Present an example of a topic sentence based on number 5 in Exercise 3:
   There are a number of ways in which technology helps students to do better research.

2. Elicit:
   - *What are the two parts of a topic sentence?*
   - *Why is the controlling idea called the "controlling idea"?* (Answer: **It controls the focus of the rest of the paragraph.**)

3. Have students discuss in pairs what the topic and controlling idea are of the sample sentence.

4. Circle the topic "ways in which technology helps students" and underline the controlling idea "do better research."

Option 2

1. Write the topic sentence from the example paragraph on page 3 on the board.

2. Circle the topic "reasons for entering higher education" and underline the controlling idea "vary."

3. Then explain the two parts of a topic sentence as questions:
   - *What is the paragraph about?* This is the topic.
   - *What does the writer want to say about the topic?* This is the controlling idea.

4. Have students go back to Exercise 3 and write a topic sentence for the topics they brainstormed.

Option 3

Refer to the diagram on page 8.

1. Elicit:
   - *Is the topic the writer's own idea?* (Answer: **No**)
   - *Is the controlling idea the writer's own idea?* (Answer: **Yes**)

2. Emphasize:
   - *The topic is not individual to the writer, but the controlling idea is the writer's own idea.*

3. Have students come up with a few more possible controlling ideas on the topic.

Option 4

When presenting the ideas at the top of page 9, about "direct and concise" topic sentences:

1. Emphasize:
   - *The topic sentence should not be too general or too specific.*

2. Elicit:
   - *Why is a topic sentence which is too general not good?*
     (Possible answers)
     - **The reader cannot get a good idea of the goal of the paragraph.**
     - **The writer risks creating a paragraph with no clear focus.**
   - *Why is a topic sentence which is too specific not good?*
     (Possible answers)
     - **It may make the reader think that the writer has limited knowledge on the topic.**
     - **The writer risks ignoring other equally related and valid points on the topic.**
     - **The writer risks not being able to develop the controlling idea because it is so specific that there is not much else to say about it.**

Exercise 4

Option 1

1. Have students do the exercise individually.

2. Have students circle the topic and underline the controlling idea in each example topic sentence.

3. In pairs or small groups, have students compare answers and explain the problems with the inappropriate topic sentences.

Option 2

1. Follow Option 1 above.

2. Then have students correct the inappropriate sentences.

3. Elicit answers.

Option 3

1. For a class of more advanced students, have them create new topic sentences which express the same idea as the correct answers.

2. Elicit answers.

Section 5 Choosing supporting points

Option 1

To check students' understanding of supporting points:

1. Write the following on the board:
   "_____ are _____ or _____ which show how the _____ is true."

   controlling idea   examples
   supporting points   reasons

2. The four words or phrases below the gapped sentence are in random order. Have students complete the gapped sentence using these words. (Answer: **Supporting points are reasons or examples which show how the controlling idea is true.**)

Option 2

1. Elicit:
   * *How do you know which supporting points to include in a paragraph?*
2. Present the three points listed at the top of page 10 for choosing supporting points.

Option 3

1. When referring to the diagrams on page 10, elicit from students other possible supporting points to support each of the controlling ideas.
2. Emphasize:
   * *Some supporting points may be more important/relevant than others. It is important for writers to be selective in deciding which supporting points to include in a paragraph.*

Option 4

1. Have students look at the example paragraph on page 3.
2. Have students draw lines to show where each supporting point begins and ends.
3. Students then label each supporting sentence as a reason or an example.
4. Emphasize:
   * *Three supporting points is a suitable number.*

Section 6 Making an outline

Option 1

1. Elicit: *Why is it necessary to make an outline?*
2. Present the three points listed at the top of page 11 about making an outline.

Option 2

1. Have students read the information in this section.
2. Then review by asking:
   * *What elements are necessary in an outline?* (Answer: **the topic, the topic sentence, and supporting points**)

Exercise 5

Option 1

1. Have students do the exercise individually.
2. In pairs or small groups, have students compare answers.

Option 2

1. In pairs or small groups, have students select one of the topics from Exercise 3 which they have notes for.
2. Have students rank the importance of each of the supporting points which they brainstormed and decide which supporting points should be used in the outline.
3. Have students combine their notes to complete the outline.

Option 3

1. Instead of using an Exercise 3 topic, have students (individually, in pairs, or in small groups) make an outline of the sample paragraph on page 3, but without looking at page 3.
2. Have students swap their outline with someone else to compare.

Review questions

Option 1

Elicit answers to the Review questions on page 12.

Option 2

1. In pairs or small groups, have students ask each other the questions on page 12.
2. Elicit answers when done.

UNIT 1

Part 2
Writing a paragraph

Supporting ideas with details

Option 1

Emphasize:

- *There is a logical "general to specific" hierarchy when presenting arguments in a paragraph:*
  - *The controlling idea is a general point about the topic.*
  - *Each supporting point shows why the controlling idea is true.*
  - *The details show specifically how the supporting point is true.*

The relationship could be illustrated as follows:

controlling idea

⌐ supporting point
  ├ detail
  └ (more details if necessary)

(Add supporting points and details as necessary)

Option 2

Demonstrate how to produce supporting details using questions with *when, where, why,* and *how.*

1. Write the following on the board:
   Topic sentence: "Living in a dormitory brings many benefits to university students."
   Supporting point: "Students can easily make friends."
   When?
   Where?
   Why?
   How?

2. Have students in small groups discuss answers to the four questions.

3. Elicit their answers.
   (Possible answers)
   - *When?*
     - **Students are surrounded by other students for almost the entire day, so students can interact with each other at any point in the day.**
   - *Where?*
     - **There are chances to talk in corridors, in cafeterias, and in communal areas.**
   - *Why?*
     - **It is easy to develop relationships because students all have the same experience in common – attending university.**

- *How?*
  - **Students can simply leave their door open and other students will often visit. Students may also just sit next to another student in a communal area and start chatting.**

Exercise 1

Option 1

Students complete this exercise individually, then compare answers with a classmate.

Option 2

Instruct students not to look back at the example on page 3, but to try to remember the details on their own.

Option 3

Have students think of their own details different from the ones in the example on page 3 to complete this outline.

Section 2
Organizing supporting sentences

Option 1

Focus students' attention on the importance of transitional words:

1. Have students close their textbooks and work with a partner to reconstruct the three supporting point sentences from the example paragraph on page 15.

2. After a few minutes, have students write their sentences on the board.

3. Check the accuracy of the sentences, especially whether or not they include the words *first, another,* and *finally.*

Option 2

Check students' understanding by asking:
- *How many supporting points are necessary in a paragraph?* (Answer: **2 or 3**)
- *What is the correct order of these elements in a paragraph – supporting point, topic sentence, details?* (Answer: **topic sentence, supporting point, details**)

Exercise 2

Option 1

1. Have students read all of the details in the right column.

2. Then have students cover the right column with their hand or a piece of paper.

3. Students in pairs or small groups are to look at the supporting points in the left column and try to recall the details which match each one *without* looking at the right column.

4. Check answers by having students close their books, then eliciting the details for each supporting point.

Option 2

After completing the exercise, challenge students to add more details under each supporting point.

Section 3 — Writing a concluding sentence

Option 1

1. Elicit:
   - *Why do some paragraphs need a concluding sentence?* (Answer: **To remind readers of the purpose of the paragraph and the main points presented**.)

2. Emphasize:
   - *The concluding sentence does not need new information.*
   - *It does need new vocabulary to describe the ideas in the paragraph without repeating the same words used in the paragraph. Therefore, students should change:*
     - *Words (e.g., "higher education" to "university")*
     - *Word forms (e.g., "vary" [verb] to "variety" [noun])*
     - *Word order (refer to topic and concluding sentence examples on page 17)*

Option 2

1. Explain:
   - *Certain transitional expressions often start a concluding sentence (e.g., "To sum up," "To summarize").*

2. Elicit a few more examples of transitional expressions which could start a concluding sentence. (Possible answers: **In conclusion, In brief, Therefore, Indeed**)

Exercise 3

Option 1

1. Have students do the exercise individually.
2. Students then compare in pairs or groups.
3. Elicit answers.

Option 2

1. Follow Option 1 above, but do not elicit answers yet.
2. Then have students work together to write a new concluding sentence based on the pair's or group's ideas. (The objective should be to pool everyone's knowledge, as changing vocabulary and structure is probably the most challenging part of writing a concluding sentence.)

Exercise 4

Option 1

If students had worked on Exercise 5, page 12 individually, have students do this exercise individually. Remind students to concentrate on changing words, word forms, and/or word order to not sound repetitive but keep the same meaning.

Option 2

If students had worked on Exercise 5, page 12 in pairs or groups, have students do this exercise in the same pairs or groups to collaboratively write a concluding sentence.

Section 4 — Choosing a title

Option 1

Emphasize:
   - *The title needs to explain the purpose of the paragraph, but it should not include information about the supporting details.*
   - *To check that capital letters are used correctly, refer to Appendix A, page 120, when students have finished writing their own titles.*

Option 2

Tell students that after writing a title, they should check that capital letters are used correctly by referring to Appendix A, page 120.

Exercise 5

Option 1

1. Have students do the exercise individually first.
2. Then have students compare answers in pairs.
3. Elicit answers when done.

Option 2

1. Have students refer back to the outline they wrote on page 12 and write down several possible titles for it (different from the wording of the topics in Exercise 3, page 7).
2. Students in pairs or small groups compare the titles they wrote and discuss why they think they are appropriate.

Option 3

Have students look at the examples in this exercise, and then ask students to decide what the rules are for using capital letters in a title. Have students refer to Appendix A (page 120) to check their ideas.

Section 5 — Writing the first draft

Option 1

In addition to the points listed on page 20, re-emphasize to students:

- *Making an outline is important because it helps writers stay focused and present their ideas logically.*
- *This is the first draft, so focus only on organizing the structure. There will be time to make changes to language (e.g., spelling, grammar, word usage) later.*

Option 2

1. Have students write a paragraph based on the outline they created in Exercise 3, page 7.

2. When done, have students swap paragraphs and evaluate the following:
   - *Does the paragraph have the three necessary components (i.e., topic sentence, supporting sentences, concluding sentence)?*
   - *Do the supporting sentences have adequate details to prove they are true?*
   - *Are transitional expressions used for the supporting sentences and concluding sentence?*

Review questions

Option 1

Elicit answers to the Review questions on page 20.

Option 2

1. Have students in pairs or small groups ask each other the questions on page 20.

2. Elicit answers when done.

UNIT 1

Part 3
Writing a coherent paragraph

Section 1 — Coherence

Option 1

1. Elicit:
   - *What does "coherence" mean?*
2. In pairs or small groups, have students discuss:
   - *What makes a piece of writing incoherent?*
3. Elicit answers and write them on the board.
4. Present the points on page 21.

Option 2

1. Have students read the explanation in the textbook.
2. Then have students close their books and summarize to each other what they read.
3. Elicit:
   - *What makes a paragraph coherent?*
4. Emphasize:
   - *A reader can understand a coherent paragraph even if it contains grammatical or vocabulary mistakes.*
   - *Therefore, when writing, students should focus on coherence first, then try to fix grammar and vocabulary later.*

Section 2 — Using conjunctions

Option 1

1. Write these two sentences on the board:
   Facebook users often have many "friends."

   People nowadays seem to have few intimate friends.
2. In pairs or small groups, have students discuss:
   - *How can these sentences be combined in a logical way?*
3. Elicit answers.
   (Possible answers)
   - **Facebook users often have many "friends," but people nowadays seem to have few intimate friends.**
   - **Although Facebook users often have many "friends," people nowadays seem to have fewer intimate friends.**

Option 2

1. Have students read the explanation in the textbook.
2. Elicit:
   - *What are possible purposes of conjunctions?*

3. Elicit:
   - *What is the difference between an independent and a dependent clause?*
4. Emphasize:
   - *Use conjunctions to connect independent and dependent clauses to write longer sentences, which are more appropriate for academic essays.*

Section 2.1 — Coordinating conjunctions

Option 1

1. Write the following coordinating conjunctions on the board:
   for and nor but or yet so
2. In pairs or small groups, have students discuss:
   - *What relationship do each of these coordinating conjunctions express?*
3. Present the ideas and examples in the table on page 23.
4. Emphasize:
   - *Using "for" as a coordinating conjunction is only commonly used in poetry, so it may seem outdated if used in an academic essay.*

Option 2

1. Refer students to the warning under the table on page 23 about starting sentences with a coordinating conjunction.
2. Explain:
   - *Starting a sentence with a coordinating conjunction is sometimes used in writing. However, beginning level students should avoid doing this because there is a high chance they will do it incorrectly (i.e., write sentence fragments).*
   - *Instead, beginning level students should concentrate on using coordinating conjunctions to combine related ideas and produce longer sentences.*

Exercise 1

Option 1

1. Have students do this exercise individually.
2. Then have students compare answers in pairs or groups.
3. Elicit answers when done.

Section 2.2 Subordinating conjunctions

Option 1

1. Refer students back to the two sentences on the board from Section 2, Option 1:
   - *Facebook users often have many "friends."*
   - *People nowadays seem to have few intimate friends.*

2. Write the subordinating conjunction "although" before the word "Facebook."

3. Elicit:
   - *Is this a complete sentence?* (Answer: **No**)
   - *What do you need to do to make this a complete sentence?* (Answer: **Combine it with the next sentence**)
   - *Where can this part* (the subordinating clause) *be placed?* (Answer: **Before or after the independent clause**)

Option 2

1. Have students look at the table of subordinating conjunctions on page 25 and cover the right side with their hand or a piece of paper.

2. Then, in pairs or small groups, have students brainstorm the subordinating clauses for each relationship type.

3. Elicit answers.

4. Emphasize:
   - *Some subordinating conjunctions have more than one function. However, the function of any conjunction should be clear from the context of the sentence.*

5. If necessary, write the following examples on the board to demonstrate how the function is clear from the context.
   - **Since rent is expensive in the center of the city, she lives outside the center and travels in to the university.** (cause)
   - **She has been renting her apartment since she entered university.** (time relationship)

Exercise 2

Option 1

1. Have students do this exercise individually.

2. Then have students compare answers in pairs or groups.

3. Elicit answers when done.

Option 2

1. Follow Option 1 above.

2. Then have students make new sentences by instructing:
   - *For each sentence, keep the first clause.*
   - *Choose one of the conjunctions you did not circle.*
   - *Create a new second clause of the sentence so the whole sentence sounds logical.*

   For example, **Some students study abroad even though they do not have much money.**

3. Elicit answers when done.

Exercise 3

Option 1

1. Have students do this exercise individually.

2. Then have students compare answers in pairs or groups.

3. Elicit answers when done.

Option 2

1. Follow Option 1 above.

2. Then have students make new sentences by instructing:
   - *For each sentence, keep the first clause.*
   - *Choose one of the conjunctions you did* not *choose originally.*
   - *Create a new second clause of the sentence so the whole sentence sounds logical.*
     (Possible answer: **While most fathers feel obliged to work full-time, some do not because the mother actually makes more money with her job.**)

3. Elicit answers when done.

Exercise 4

Option 1

1. Have students do this exercise individually, then compare answers in pairs or groups.

2. Elicit answers when done.

Option 2

1. Have students work in pairs or small groups to discuss ideas and then collaboratively write answers.

2. Elicit answers when done.

Option 3

1. Have students choose two subordinating conjunctions from the table on page 25 that they rarely use in their own writing. Challenge students to use these in the exercise.

2. Elicit answers when done.

Section 3 Using transitional expressions

Option 1

1. Have students open their book to page 123 and cover the right three columns with a piece of paper.

2. Then, in pairs or small groups, have students brainstorm the transitional expressions for each function.

3. Elicit answers when done.

Option 2

1. Have students read the example sentences under "Listing ideas."

2. Then have students close their book and, in pairs, try to recall the sentences, paying special attention to the use of the transitional expressions.

3. Repeat the same process for the rest of the functions.

4. Emphasize:
   - *Transitional expressions are important because they make the ideas the writer presents easy to follow by showing how they are related.*
   - *Using a greater variety of transitional expressions is an easy way to improve writing style.*

Exercise 5

Option 1

1. Have students do this exercise individually, then compare answers in pairs or groups.

2. Remind students to read the whole sentence before deciding the appropriate transitional expression.

3. Elicit answers when done.

Option 2

To encourage use of a wide range of different expressions:

1. Have students look at page 123 and circle the transitional expressions they have never used or rarely use.

2. Then have students try to use these expressions when they do this exercise.

Section 4 — Avoiding run-on sentences and sentence fragments

This section is about raising students' awareness of mistakes that can cause readers to misunderstand. The amount of time you spend on this activity should reflect how much of a problem this is for your students.

Section 4.1 — Run-on sentences

Option 1

1. Elicit:
   - *What does it mean to "run-on"?*

2. Refer students back to the two sentences on the board from Section 2, Option 1, but erase the period after "friends" so the sentences look like this:
   Facebook users often have many "friends" People nowadays seem to have few intimate friends.

3. Ask students to imagine this is all one sentence.

4. Elicit:
   - *What is the problem with this?*

5. Elicit:
   - *What can you do to fix this?*

Option 2

To test students' understanding of these ideas:

1. Write the following example on the board:
   Some students who study foreign languages decide to go overseas to study, however most students do not have the time or money to do this.

2. Individually or in pairs, have students identify the mistake in the above sentence and write two possible correct sentences.
   (Possible answers)
   - **Some students who study foreign languages decide to go overseas to study, but most students do not have the time or money to do this.**
   - **Some students who study foreign languages decide to go overseas to study. However, most students do not have the time or money to do this.**

3. Emphasize:
   - *In general, longer sentences are more academic, so it is advisable to choose this option rather than separating into two shorter sentences.*

Section 4.2 — Sentence fragments

Option 1

1. Elicit:
   - *What does "fragment" mean?*

2. Have students look at each of the incomplete sentences on page 30, but not at the correct sentences on pages 30 and 31.

3. For each sentence, elicit:
   - *What is the problem in this sentence?*

4. For each sentence, elicit:
   - *What are some words I can add to make this a complete sentence?*

5. Present the three points on how to correct sentence fragments.

Option 2

To test students' understanding of these ideas:

1. Write the following example on the board:
   Many students say that university is a beneficial social experience. As they can meet many different kinds of people.

2. Ask students to write two alternative (correct) versions of this sentence:
   (Possible answers)
   - **Many students say that university is a beneficial social experience, as they can meet many different kinds of people.**
   - **Many students say that university is a beneficial social experience. This is because they can meet many different kinds of people.**

3. Emphasize again:
   - *In general, longer sentences are more academic, so it is advisable to choose this*

option rather than separating into two shorter sentences.

Exercise 6

Option 1

1. Have students do this exercise individually, then compare answers in pairs or groups.
2. Elicit answers when done.

Option 2

1. Follow Option 1 above.
2. For the sentences with mistakes, ask students to make two different corrections, one which divides the sentence into two parts and one which is a single sentence.

Review questions

Option 1

Elicit answers to the Review questions on page 31.

Option 2

1. Have students in pairs or small groups ask each other the questions on page 31.
2. Elicit answers when done.

Part 4
Editing a paragraph

Section 1 — Academic writing style

Option 1

1. In pairs or small groups, have students briefly discuss the following:
   - *What is the difference between spoken and written English?*

   AND/OR
   - *How is academic writing different from personal or informal writing?*
2. Present the points on page 32.

Option 2

1. Have students read the explanation and table in the textbook.
2. Then have students close their books and summarize to each other what they read.
3. Elicit answers to the following questions:
   - *What are three things academic writing should be?*
   - *What are the DO's and DON'Ts to be formal?*
   - *What are the DO's and DON'Ts to be objective?*
   - *What are the DO's and DON'Ts to be logical?*
4. Emphasize:
   - *Failure to use academic style may result in the reader not taking the writer's work seriously.*
   - *Therefore, check this advice on page 32 again each time before writing an academic essay.*

Exercise 1

Option 1

1. Have students read the two paragraphs.
2. Then in pairs or groups, have students discuss their answers to the questions.
3. Remind students to refer to the guidelines on page 32 in the textbook when they are discussing what makes Paragraph B less academic.

Option 2

To make the exercise more challenging:
1. Have students underline the parts in Paragraph B that are not academic.
2. Then in pairs or small groups, have students discuss how to change the sentences so they are more academic.
3. Remind students to refer to the guidelines on page 32 in the textbook when they are discussing how to change the problems with Paragraph B.

Section 2 — Editing the first draft

Option 1

1. Elicit:
   - *Why is editing an important process when writing an academic essay?*
2. Present the points on page 34.

Option 2

1. Have students read the explanation in the textbook.
2. Then have students close their books and summarize to each other what they read.
3. Elicit answers to the following questions:
   - *What should you do when editing your own essay?* (Answer on page 34)
   - *What is the advantage of peer editing?* (Answer on page 34)
4. Emphasize:
   - *Academic writing is rarely something which can be done with just one draft.*
   - *Writing should be seen as a process of production and revision.*
   - *Students should expect to review their work before submitting it.*
   - *Get into the habit of asking for peer editing because it is much easier for students to get feedback from a classmate than a teacher or professor, who may be too busy to give regular feedback.*

Section 3 — Editing a paragraph

Option 1

1. Have students read the editing checklist in the textbook.
2. Then have students close their books and in pairs or small groups recall what they read.
3. Elicit answers to the following:
   - *When editing, what should you do in the first reading?*
   - *What are questions you can ask about content?*
   - *What are questions you can ask about organization?*
   - *What should you do in the second reading?*
   - *What are questions you can ask about grammar and style?*

4. Explain:
   - *The order of the elements in the checklist follows the importance of each – content is first, as it is the most important, then organization, then grammar and style.*
   - *The final section on comments is for anything else not covered by the preceding questions.*
   - *Do not just view editing as "fault finding." The checklist contains a section on "Strengths." One of the benefits of peer editing is that students can see good examples of how to do things right, and gain ideas for their own writing.*

Exercise 2

Option 1

1. Have students individually edit the paragraph, focusing only on the questions for content and organization first.

2. Then in pairs or small groups, have students compare their edits.

3. Next, have students individually edit for grammar and style.

4. Then in pairs or small groups, have students compare their edits.

5. Elicit some edits from a few students.

Option 2

If students wrote a paragraph based on Exercise 3 (page 7) or Exercise 5 (page 12) in Unit 1 Part 1:

1. In pairs or small groups, have students swap the paragraph they wrote and peer edit each other's paragraph.

2. When done, have students explain their edits to the writer.

3. Emphasize:
   - *Finding weaknesses is only the first step of editing. Students should go the extra step and make corrections to improve the weaknesses.*
   - *When peer editing, comment also on positives. Editing should be seen as a chance to identify the points which make good writing.*

Review questions

Option 1

Elicit answers to the Review questions on page 36.

Option 2

1. Have students in pairs or small groups ask each other the questions on page 36.

2. Elicit answers when done.

UNIT 2

Part 1
From a paragraph to an essay

Section 1 — What is an essay?

Option 1

1. Have students read the explanation in the textbook.
2. Then have students close their books and summarize to each other what they read.
3. Elicit answers to the following questions:
   - *How many topics does an essay discuss?* (Answer: **1**)
   - *What are the three parts of an essay, and what is their correct order?* (Answer: **introductory paragraph, body paragraphs, concluding paragraph**)

Section 2 — The structure of an essay

Option 1

1. Have students read pages 39 and 40.
2. Then have students close their books and summarize to each other what they read.
3. Elicit answers to the following:
   - *How are a paragraph and an essay similar?*
   - *What are the two parts of an introductory paragraph?*
   - *What are the three parts of a body paragraph?*
   - *What are the three parts of a concluding paragraph?*

Option 2

1. Explain that the essay can be thought of in basic terms as follows:
   - *The introductory paragraph explains the objective of the essay.*
   - *The body paragraphs achieve the objective of the essay.*
   - *The concluding paragraph emphasizes the main points of the essay.*
2. Emphasize:
   - *Students must include all of the elements in the graphic on page 39 to write an effective essay.*

Option 3

Explain that the elements of a paragraph that students studied in Unit 1 can be compared with the elements of an essay.

   - *The topic sentence of a paragraph has a similar function to the introductory paragraph.*
   - *The supporting sentences of a paragraph have a similar function to the body paragraphs.*

   - *The concluding sentence of a paragraph has a similar function to the concluding paragraph.*

Exercise 1

Option 1

1. Have students read the essay in full, at their own pace.
2. Then in pairs or small groups, have students summarize the essay to each other.
3. Have students discuss the answers to the questions in pairs or small groups.

Option 2

1. Have students do question 1 individually.
2. Elicit answers.
3. Have students do question 2 individually with the following instructions:
   - *For the introductory paragraph, draw a box around the building sentences and underline the thesis statement.*
   - *For each of the body paragraphs, underline the topic sentences, draw a box around the supporting sentences, and underline the concluding sentence.*
   - *For the concluding paragraph, underline the restatement of the thesis, draw a box around the summary of the body paragraphs, and underline the final thought.*
4. When done, have students in pairs or small groups compare their answers.
5. Elicit answers.
6. In pairs or small groups, have students discuss question 3.
7. Emphasize:
   - *The answer to these two questions is key information about the essay which should be included in the thesis statement.*

Section 3 — Writing a thesis statement

Option 1

1. Have students read page 42.
2. Then have students close their books and summarize to each other what they read.
3. Elicit answers to the following:
   - *Why is the thesis statement the most important part of the essay?*
     (Possible answers)
     - **It answers the essay question completely.**
     - **By reading the thesis, readers will know what the purpose and content of the essay are.**

- *What are the elements of a thesis statement?*
  (Answer: **the topic, writer's opinion, main ideas**)

Option 2

1. Explain the three major components of the thesis statement with questions:
   - *What is the essay about? The topic.*
   - *What does the writer think about the topic? The writer's opinion.*
   - *Why does the writer have this opinion? The main ideas.*

2. Then refer to the sample essay and say:
   - *The essay is about why students go to university.*
   - *The writer believes that students go to university for a variety of reasons.*
   - *The writer's opinion is that the three reasons are: academic interest, future career, and social life.*

Exercise 2

Option 1

1. Have students do this individually.

2. In pairs or small groups, have students compare answers.

3. Write sample answers on the board for students to check. (See answer key)

Option 2

1. Have students sit in pairs and decide who is student A and who is student B.

2. For number 1, have student A write a thesis statement with a colon, and student B write a thesis statement without a colon.

3. Then have students compare answers.

4. For number 2, switch students' roles.

5. For number 3, students can choose which style they prefer.

Section 4 | **Writing the topic sentences of body paragraphs**

Option 1

1. Have students read the explanation on page 44.

2. Then have students close their books and summarize to each other what they read.

3. Elicit:
   - *What are the two parts of a topic sentence?*
   - *What is repeated in all of the topic sentences in an essay?* (Answer: **The topic and writer's opinion**)
   - *Why is the topic and writer's opinion repeated in all of the topic sentences?* (Answer: **To remind the reader what the essay is about**)
   - *What does the controlling idea do?* (Answer: **It tells the reader which of the main ideas from the thesis is being developed in that paragraph**)

Option 2

1. When students have read page 44, test their understanding with these "true or false" statements:
   - *The "topic" and "writer's opinion on the topic" in a topic sentence should be the same as the "topic" and "opinion on the topic" in the thesis statement.* (**True**)
   - *The controlling ideas in the topic sentences should be different from the main ideas in the thesis statement.* (**False – the controlling ideas should be the same as the main ideas in the thesis**)
   - *The controlling ideas in the body paragraphs should be in the same order as the main ideas presented in the thesis statement.* (**True**)
   - *The controlling idea should be the same in each topic sentence.* (**False – it should be different in the topic sentence of each body paragraph**)

2. Emphasize:
   - *The topic sentences need to show the relationship of the paragraph to the thesis statement: each of the two elements of a topic sentence relates to a part of the thesis.*
   - *The topic and the writer's opinion can be very similar, and in some instances may overlap. For example, the topic of "reasons for going to university" and the opinion "there are a variety of reasons why students go to university" contain similar words and ideas.*

Exercise 3

Option 1

1. Have students do the exercise individually.

2. Then in pairs or small groups, have students discuss their answers.

3. Elicit answers.

Option 2

1. Follow Option 1 above.

2. Then have students write a corrected version of each topic sentence without looking back at page 44.

3. Elicit answers.

Section 5 | **Transitional expressions and avoiding repetition**

Option 1

1. Have students read the explanation on page 46.

2. Then have students close their books and summarize to each other what they read.

3. Elicit:
   - *What do transitional expressions do?* (Answer: **Indicate the order of the main ideas and the beginning of a new paragraph**)
   - *What are some other transitional expressions which could begin a paragraph?* (Possible answers: **Firstly, One reason, Secondly, Another reason, Thirdly, A third reason**)

- *How can you avoid repetition in topic sentences?* (Answer: **Change the words but keep the same meaning**)

Option 2

1. Have students look at the thesis statement and topic sentences at the bottom of page 46.

2. In pairs or small groups, have students discuss:
   - *How exactly did the writer avoid repetition in the three topic sentences?*

3. Elicit answers.
   (Answers)
   - **Body paragraph 1 topic sentence, changed "go to" to "attend"**
   - **Body paragraph 2 topic sentence, changed the word order**
   - **Body paragraph 3 topic sentence, changed "university" to "school" and changed "go to" to "stay in … for another four years"**

4. Emphasize:
   - *Repeating exactly the same words is poor essay style.*
   - *To avoid repetition, students should use different words in each topic sentence from those used in the thesis statement.*
   - *However, students do not need to make changes to every single word. They may choose to change any of the following:*
     - *Words ("go to" to "attend")*
     - *Word form ("go to" to "going to")*
     - *Word order ("Students go to university for a variety of reasons" to "reasons for going to university")*
   - *When making any changes, it is important to keep a similar meaning to that expressed in the thesis.*

Exercise 4

Option 1

1. Have students do the exercise individually.

2. Then in pairs or small groups, have students discuss their answers.

3. Elicit answers.

Option 2

1. In pairs or small groups, have students work collaboratively to write the topic sentences.

2. Elicit answers.

Exercise 5

Option 1

1. Have students do the exercise individually.

2. Then in pairs or small groups, have students discuss their answers.

3. Elicit answers.

Option 2

1. In pairs or small groups, have students work collaboratively to write the topic sentences.

2. Elicit answers.

Section 6 — Making an essay outline

Option 1

Elicit:
- *What should you do before writing an essay?* (Answer: **Make an outline**)
- *Why is this step necessary?* (Answer)
  - **Before writing, helps the writer form ideas and structure them logically.**
  - **While writing, gives guidance by helping the writer stay focused on supporting the thesis.**

Option 2

1. Have students read the explanation on page 48.

2. Then elicit:
   - *What are the four elements in an essay outline?* (Answer: **Topic, thesis statement, topic sentences, supporting points**)
   - *When you make an essay outline, which of the following elements must be a complete sentence?*
     Topic
     Thesis statement
     Topic sentences
     Supporting points
     (Answer: **Everything except the supporting points**)

3. Emphasize:
   - *An essay outline has the same purpose as a paragraph outline (which students studied in Unit 1). It helps writers form their ideas and structure them logically.*
   - *This will save time because the essay will be easier to write, compared with just sitting down and immediately beginning writing with no guidance.*
   - *An outline also allows students to see the essay as a whole, which gives them confidence because they know what to say in the essay.*

Exercise 6

Option 1

1. Have students do the exercise individually.

2. Then in pairs or small groups, have students compare their answers.

3. Elicit answers.

Option 2

1. In pairs or small groups, have students try to recall the missing supporting points without looking back at the model essay on page 41.

2. Elicit answers.

For Option 1 or 2

Remind students:
- *The supporting points should only be the key details, not complete sentences.*

Option 1

Elicit:
- *What are the different brainstorming techniques studied in Unit 1?*

Option 2

1. Have students do the exercise individually by instructing:
   - *First, brainstorm your ideas.*
   - *Then fill in the outline.*
2. Tell students:
   - *Although there are only two lines for the supporting points in each paragraph, write more than two points if necessary.*
3. When done, in pairs or small groups, have students compare their outlines.

Option 3

1. In pairs or small groups, have students work collaboratively by instructing:
   - *First, brainstorm your ideas.*
   - *Then fill in the outline.*
2. Tell students:
   - *Although there are only two lines for the supporting points in each paragraph, write more than two points if necessary.*
3. When done, have the student pairs/groups show their outline to another pair/group.

Option 4

1. Have students work in pairs or small groups.
2. Assign half the pairs/groups essay topic 3, and half the pairs/groups essay topic 4.
3. Instruct the students to:
   - *First, brainstorm your ideas.*
   - *Then fill in the outline.*
4. Tell students:
   - *Although there are only two lines for the supporting points in each paragraph, write more than two points if necessary.*
5. After completing the outline, have pairs or groups who made an outline for the same essay topic compare their outlines.

For Option 2, 3, or 4

To elicit answers:
1. Select a few students and have them read their outline.
2. Give comments on the thesis statement and topic sentences based on:
   - Structure
   - Word choice
   - Grammar

Review questions

Option 1

Elicit answers to the Review questions on page 51.

Option 2

1. Have students in pairs or small groups ask each other the questions on page 51.
2. Elicit answers when done.

Section 1 — Developing body paragraphs

Option 1

1. Elicit:
   - *What does it mean to "develop a paragraph"?*
2. Have students read the explanation and example body paragraph on page 52.

Option 2

To reinforce the idea of "developing body paragraphs":
1. After reading the sample paragraph, have students close their books or cover the paragraph with their hand.
2. Then elicit:
   - *What is the topic sentence?*
3. When students give the correct answer, write the controlling idea in abbreviated form on the board, e.g.,
   - *study subject in depth*
4. Then elicit:
   - *What is supporting point 1?*
   - *What details are given for that?*
   - *What is supporting point 2?*
   - *What details are given for that?*
   - *What is supporting point 3?*
   - *What details are given for that?*
5. As students give the correct answer for each question, write it on the board in abbreviated form next to the abbreviated controlling idea, e.g.:

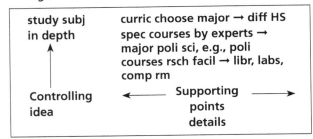

6. Then draw arrows from each supporting point back to the controlling idea, e.g.:

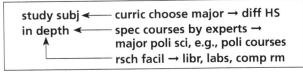

7. Emphasize:
   - *This paragraph is well developed. There are three supporting points, and each is explained further with details.*

   - *In a well-developed paragraph, it should not be difficult for readers to recall what the supporting points are because they should all be closely related to the controlling idea in the topic sentence.*

8. Emphasize:
   - *A body paragraph needs to be developed with enough information to show why the controlling idea of the topic sentence is true.*
   - *In general, three supporting points are usually enough for this. Two points may be enough if they are strong and well supported with details.*
   - *Each supporting point must be further explained with details.*

Note:
- For supporting point 3, the details are in the same sentence ("… such as libraries, laboratories, and computer rooms.").
- The last sentence of the paragraph is the concluding sentence.

Exercise 1

Option 1

1. Have students do the exercise individually.
2. Then in pairs or small groups, have students compare their answers.
3. Elicit answers.

Option 2

1. In pairs or small groups, have students try to recall the missing supporting points without looking back at the model essay on page 41.
2. Elicit answers.

Emphasize:
- *Students should use the essay outline on page 53 as a model when they write their own essay.*

Exercise 2

Option 1

1. Have students do the exercise individually.
2. Then in pairs or small groups, have students compare their outlines.

Option 2

1. In pairs or small groups, have students work collaboratively to complete the outline.
2. When done, have the student pairs/groups show their outline to another pair/group.

For Option 1 or 2

Elicit answers from the students. Write them on the board to show the variety of details that could be used to explain supporting points.

Section 2 **Writing an introductory paragraph**

There is a lot of information in this section, and it can more manageably be broken down into three stages.

Stage 1

Option 1

1. Have students read the explanation on page 55 and example at the top of page 56.
2. Then elicit:
   - *What are the two elements of an introductory paragraph and what order should they appear in?*
     (Answer: **Building sentences, then thesis statement**)
   - *What should the building sentences do?*
     (Answer: **Introduce the essay topic and provide background information on the essay topic**)
   - *How should the building sentences be organized?* (Answer: **From general to specific information**)
   - *What should the thesis statement do?* (Answer: **Present the writer's opinion about the topic and main ideas of the essay**)

Option 2

To emphasize the purpose of building sentences:
1. Have students read only the explanation on page 55.
2. Elicit:
   - *In the sample paragraph on page 55, what information do you learn in the building sentences?*
3. Then have students look at the flow chart at the top of page 56.
4. Emphasize:
   - *Building sentences should present background information on the topic as it is related to the thesis. This often includes any combination of:*
     - *historical information,*
     - *statistical information,*
     - *information on the present situation.*
5. Then present the following:
   - *The building sentences in the sample paragraph explain the present situation.*
   - *Possible historical information could be:*
     "In the past, only elite and literate students could attend university. However, from the 20th century, more students were able to enter university because ..."
   - *Possible statistical information could be:*
     "Research shows that the number of students attending university is steadily increasing. In 1950, the percentage of high school students who moved on to university was 50 percent. Today, that percentage is ..."

Stage 2

Option 1

1. Have students read the explanation and example of the introductory paragraph on page 56.
2. Then have students compare the inappropriate example on page 56 with the appropriate example on page 55.
3. In pairs or small groups, have students discuss:
   - *Why is the sample paragraph on page 55 better?*
4. Elicit answers. (Answer: **Because the building sentences, especially the opening sentence, are more closely related to the thesis than in the paragraph on page 56.**)

Option 2

1. Have students read only the sample introductory paragraph on page 56.
2. Then in pairs or small groups, have students compare the sample on page 56 with the one on page 55 and discuss:
   - *Which introductory paragraph is better? Why?*
3. Elicit answers. (Answer: **The first one, because the building sentences, especially the opening sentence, are more closely related to the thesis.**)

Stage 3

1. Have students read the explanation and examples on page 57.
2. Write the following example on the board:
   Living situations of university students can be classified into three types: living with their families, living in a dormitory, and living alone in an apartment.
3. Elicit:
   - *What themes are in this thesis?* (Answer: **education and accommodation**)
4. Explain:
   - *The opening sentence could therefore discuss education, accommodation, or even both.*
5. Write the following example on the board:
   - *A student's living situation is an important part of their university experience.*
6. Elicit:
   - *What words in the opening sentence express the theme of "education"?* (Answer: **student's, university**)
   - *What words in the opening sentence express the theme of "accommodation"?* (Answer: **living situation**)
7. Emphasize:
   - *An opening sentence should be general but closely related to the thesis. This will help keep the introductory paragraph focused.*

Exercise 3

Option 1

1. Have students do the exercise individually.

2. Then in pairs or small groups, have students compare their answers.

3. Elicit answers.

Option 2

1. In pairs or small groups, have students work collaboratively to complete the exercise.

2. Elicit answers.

For Option 1 or 2

Emphasize:
- *Read all of the sentences before starting to put them in the correct order.*
- *Building sentences should move from general to specific, so when doing this exercise, pay attention to which sentences contain examples, as these should be later in the paragraph.*

Exercise 4

Option 1

1. In pairs or small groups, have students brainstorm ideas and discuss how they can complete this task.

2. Then have each pair/group choose a writer to complete the task.

3. The other students should help with spelling, vocabulary, and correction of errors.

4. When done, select a few pairs/groups to write their building sentences on the board.

5. Then compare the similarities and differences between each set of sentences.

Option 2

1. Assign pairs or small groups and have each pair/group choose a writer to complete the task.

2. Assign half the class number 1, and the other half number 2.

3. Have students brainstorm ideas and discuss how they can complete this task.

4. When done, select one pair/group who did number 1 and another who did number 2 to write their building sentences on the board.

5. The whole class can then compare their sentences with these models.

Section 3 Writing a concluding paragraph

1. Have students read the brief explanation at the top of page 60.

2. To check their understanding, draw a diagram on the board. First, draw a box with five lines in it. The box represents the concluding paragraph and the lines represent the sentences.

3. Then elicit:
- *What is the first sentence?* (Answer: **Restatement of the thesis**)
- *What are the second, third, and fourth sentences?* (Answer: **Summary of the body paragraphs**)

- *What is the fifth sentence?* (Answer: **Final thought**)

4. As students give each answer correctly, fill in the box on the appropriate line. Eventually, the box should look like this:

restatement of the thesis
summary of the first body paragraph
summary of the second body paragraph
summary of the third body paragraph
final thought

5. Emphasize:
- *The concluding paragraph should not contain new information.*
- *The function is to remind the reader of the important points in the essay.*

Section 3.1 Restatement of the thesis

Option 1

1. Have students read the information on page 60.

2. Elicit:
- *What are some rules about the restatement of the thesis?*
   (Answer)
   - **Use different sentence structures and words when restating the topic of the essay and the writer's opinion.**
   - **Begin with a transitional expression.**

Option 2

To practice changing key vocabulary and altering the structure of the sentence:

1. Write the following thesis on the board (from Exercise 4, number 1, page 59):
   Common causes of stress among university students can be classified into three types: assignment deadlines, grades, and job hunting.

2. Then elicit:
- *What is the topic and writer's opinion?*
   (Answer: **The topic is common causes of stress and the writer's opinion is that they can be divided into three types.**)

3. Then focus students on the two different parts they need to restate by underlining them:
   Common causes of stress among university students can be classified into three types: assignment deadlines, grades, and job hunting.

4. Explain:
- *When restating the thesis, the simplest thing to do is to change the order of these two elements.*
- *Then alter some of the main vocabulary.*

5. Write the following example on the board:
   To sum up, it is possible to describe three different types of things which frequently cause university students to feel stress.

Emphasize:
- *When restating the thesis, only restate the topic and opinion.*
- *The three main ideas from the thesis statement are the same as the ideas in the body paragraphs, so these will be summarized in the restatement of the main ideas (the next part of the concluding paragraph).*
- *When trying to find synonyms to replace certain vocabulary, using a dictionary or thesaurus can be risky. Although synonyms have similar meanings, they are often not interchangeable. For example, "antique" and "old" are synonyms, but calling an "old person" an "antique person" is incorrect. In general, it is better for students to use vocabulary they are already familiar with.*

Section 3.2 Restatement of the main ideas

Option 1

1. Have students read the explanation on pages 60–61.
2. Elicit:
   - *What are some rules about the restatement of the main ideas?*
   (Answer)
     - **Restate the topic sentences of the body paragraphs.**
     - **There should be three sentences restating the main ideas in the concluding paragraph.**
     - **Use different sentence structures and words when restating.**

Option 2

1. Have students read the "restatements of the topic sentences" example at the top of page 61.
2. In pairs or small groups, have students discuss:
   - *What was changed in these sentences to restate the body paragraph topic sentences?*
3. Elicit answers.
   (Answer)
   - *Sentence 1: "students" "them," "study" "explore," "subject" "academic field"*
   - *Sentence 2: "going to" "attend," "advantage" "leads to a better," "career" "job market"*
   - *Sentence 3: word order was changed: "stay in school for another four years" "go to university," "enjoying an active social life" "meet people," "making friends" "develop friendships"*

Exercise 5

Option 1

1. Have students do the exercise individually.
2. Then in pairs or small groups, have students compare their restatements.
3. Elicit answers and assess quality by commenting on the following criteria:

- *Change of words or sentence structure*
- *Appropriateness of synonyms or grammar*
- *Maintaining the original meaning*

Option 2

1. In pairs or small groups, have students work collaboratively to complete the exercise.
2. When done, select a few pairs/groups to write their restatements on the board.
3. Then compare the similarities and differences between each set of restatements.

Section 3.3 The final thought

Option 1

1. Have students read the explanation and examples on page 64.
2. Then have students close their books and summarize to each other what they read.
3. Elicit answers to the following questions:
   - *What is the purpose of the final thought?* (Answer: **To leave the reader with a strong impression and encourage the reader to think about the topic further**)
   - *What are two kinds of final thought?* (Answer: **An overall opinion and a prediction**)
   - *What should you not do in the final thought?* (Answer: **Do not use "I" or "you"; do not introduce new ideas or details**)

Option 2

1. Write the following sentence on the board: *Students going to university have a lot to think about.*
2. Elicit:
   - *Why is this not a good final thought?*
3. Emphasize:
   - *This sentence is too general and obvious.*
   - *A final thought should not be a general statement that everyone can agree with. It should be precise and thought provoking.*
4. Then write the following sentence on the board: *Students who don't think about the benefits of university are just stupid and just wasting their time.*
5. Elicit:
   - *Why is this not a good final thought?*
6. Emphasize:
   - *This is too subjective and does not sound academic.*
   - *Even when expressing an opinion, the final thought should still be academic – i.e., objective.*
7. Then write the following and explain that this is a more suitable final thought: *It is important for students to realize the many different aspects of university and decide what they want to gain from the experience.*

Exercise 6

Option 1

1. Have students do the exercise individually.
2. Then in pairs or small groups, have students discuss their rewrites.
3. Elicit answers.

Option 2

1. In pairs or small groups, have students work collaboratively to write the rewrites.
2. Then have each pair/group compare their answers with another pair/group.
3. Elicit answers.

After Option 1 or 2

Another way to check answers:
1. Have a few students come up to the board to write their final thoughts.
2. Compare similarities and differences.

Review questions

Option 1

Elicit answers to the Review questions on page 65.

Option 2

1. Have students in pairs or small groups ask each other the questions on page 65.
2. Elicit answers when done.

UNIT 2

Part 3
Editing an essay

Section 1   Using pronouns

Option 1

1. Have students read pages 66 and 67.
2. Then elicit:
   - *Why are pronouns useful in essays?* (Answer: **Help avoid repetition, improve coherence**)
   - *How should academic writing be written?* (Answer: **From a third person point of view**)
   - *What does a "third person" point of view mean?* (Answer: **Writer and reader view the topic from the outside**)
   - *How do writers write in the third person?* (Answer: **Use pronouns like "he," "she," "they," "one," not "I," "we," or "you"**)

Option 2

(Before doing option 1)

1. In pairs or small groups, have students discuss:
   - *What is the difference between a text message to a friend and writing an academic essay?*
2. Elicit answers.
3. Emphasize:
   - *Different kinds of writing have different styles. In order to be effective, it is important to follow the style which is appropriate for the writing which you are doing.*

Option 3

To show how pronouns are useful:

1. Write the following sentences on the board:
   Students in university have a variety of facilities students can use.
   Students often use the library to study or do research.
   For example, students may use computers in the library.
   Using computers in the library is helpful for students because computers are the most common way for students to do research.
2. Elicit:
   - *What is wrong with the style of these sentences?* (Answer: **Repetition of the same words. Pronouns needed.**)
3. In pairs or small groups, have students discuss:
   - *Where can these sentences be fixed so they do not sound repetitive?*
4. Elicit answers:
   (Answers)
   - **Students in university have a variety of facilities** ~~students~~ <u>they</u> **can use.**
   - ~~Students~~ <u>They</u> **often use the library to study or do research.**

   - For example, ~~students~~ <u>they</u> may use computers in the library.
   - ~~Using computers in the library~~ <u>This</u> is helpful for students because computers are the most common way for ~~students~~ <u>them</u> to do research.

5. Emphasize:
   - *Overusing a pronoun is just as bad as overusing the original word or phrase. Use both enough times so the sentences do not sound repetitive.*

Option 4

To demonstrate writing in the "third person":

1. Write the following sentences on the board:
   You are becoming obese because of a variety of reasons.
   I am becoming obese because of a variety of reasons.
   We are becoming obese because of a variety of reasons.
   People are becoming obese because of a variety of reasons.
2. Elicit:
   - *Which is the most academic sounding sentence?* (Answer: **"People are ... " because it is written in the third person**)
3. Emphasize:
   - *Using inappropriate language for an academic essay creates a bad impression on the reader and means that the reader is unlikely to take the information seriously.*
   - *The third person is used in academic writing because information viewed from the outside is presented as an objective truth. This is much stronger than a subjective style which presents information as a personal opinion or based on personal experience.*

Exercise 1

Option 1

1. Have students do the exercise individually.
2. Then in pairs or small groups, have students compare their answers.
3. Elicit answers.

Option 2

1. In pairs or small groups, have students work collaboratively to complete the exercise.
2. Elicit answers.

Section 2 Editing an essay

Option 1

1. Have students read the explanation and look at the checklist on page 69.

2. Then elicit:
   - *How many times should you read an essay when editing it?*
   - *What should you check during each reading?*

3. Elicit answers:
   (Answer)
   There should be two readings minimum:
   - **First reading is to check for content and organization.**
   - **Second reading is for grammar and style.**

Option 2

1. Before looking at the textbook, in pairs or small groups, have students discuss:
   - *What do you need to check when editing an essay?*

2. Elicit answers. (Answer: **Content, organization, grammar and style**)

3. Then write on the board:
   Content
   Organization
   Grammar and style

4. In pairs or small groups, discuss:
   - *What questions should you ask about each when editing?*

5. Elicit answers.

6. Refer students to the Essay Editing Checklist on page 69.

7. Emphasize:
   - *The checklist presents the more important things first – checking for content, then organization, then grammar and style.*
   - *Don't worry too much about grammar. Successfully completing an essay is more about content and organization than grammar.*

Exercise 2

Option 1

1. Have students do part 1 of the exercise individually.

2. When done, in pairs or small groups, have students compare their answers.

3. Elicit answers.

4. Then have students do part 2 of the exercise individually.

5. When done, in pairs or small groups, have students compare their answers.

6. Elicit answers.

Option 2

1. In pairs or small groups, have students work collaboratively to complete part 1 of the exercise.

2. Have each pair/group compare their comments with another pair's/group's.

3. Elicit answers.

4. In pairs or small groups, have students work collaboratively to complete part 2 of the exercise.

5. Have each pair/group compare their edits/comments with another pair's/group's.

6. Elicit answers.

For both Option 1 and 2

Emphasize:
- *This exercise is not just about finding mistakes. It is important to suggest actual ways to make improvements.*
- *Focus on all parts of the essay, as all parts may contain mistakes and need improving.*
- *Look for positive things as well. Comment on what is successful in the essay.*

Review questions

Option 1

Elicit answers to the Review questions on page 70.

Option 2

1. Have students in pairs or small groups ask each other the questions on page 70.

2. Elicit answers when done.

UNIT 3

Part 1
Paraphrasing and summarizing

Option 1

1. Introduce the topic. In pairs or small groups, have students discuss:
   - *Why do you need to include other people's ideas in an essay?*
2. Elicit answers.
   (Possible answers)
   - **They provide valuable support to arguments.**
   - **Readers have no reason to trust a student's opinion, since the student is neither famous nor credible. Ideas from reliable outside sources are needed to strengthen the credibility of what the student is saying.**

Option 2

1. Have students read page 72 and the table at the top of page 73.
2. In pairs or small groups, with books closed, have students summarize to each other what they read.
3. Elicit:
   - *Why do you need to include other people's ideas in an essay?* (Answer: **They are necessary to support the writer's opinion.**)
   - *What are ways to add information from outside sources in an essay?* (Answer: **quoting, paraphrasing, summarizing**)
   - *What is the difference between these methods?*
     (Answer)
     - **quoting = exact words in quotation marks**
     - **paraphrasing = writer's own words, all details from source and same length as original**
     - **summarizing = writer's own words, most important ideas from and much shorter than original**

Section 2   Paraphrasing

Option 1

1. Have students read page 73.
2. In pairs or small groups, books closed, have students summarize to each other what they read.
3. Elicit:
   - *What are the rules for paraphrasing?*
     (Answer)
     - **Write in your own words**
     - **Keep the same details as the original**
     - **Do not change ideas from the original**
     - **Do not remove or add new ideas**

- *What is shared language?* (Answer: **Words which should not be changed because they cannot effectively be expressed in any other way**)

Option 2

1. In pairs or small groups, have students think of two more examples of each of the types of shared language.
2. Elicit answers.
   (Possible answers)
   - **Proper nouns: Paris, The Statue of Liberty**
   - **Common nouns that are difficult to reword: language, factory**
   - **Technical terms: internet server, thesis statement**
   - **Numbers and dates: 8:30 a.m., 1776**

Option 3

1. Have students look at the three paraphrases at the bottom of page 73.
2. In pairs or small groups, have students discuss:
   - *What is wrong with paraphrases a and b?*
3. Elicit answers.
4. Present the explanation at the top of page 74.
5. Emphasize:
   - *Identifying shared language is important when paraphrasing. Doing this first will save time because students will know what they do not need to change in a paraphrase (or summary).*
   - *When paraphrasing, focus on changing words, word forms, and sentence structure. This is similar to the advice presented before in the textbook about writing a concluding sentence in a body paragraph, and restating the thesis and main ideas in the concluding paragraph.*

Exercise 1

Option 1

1. Have students do the exercise individually.
2. Then in pairs or small groups, have students compare their answers.
3. Elicit answers.

Option 2

1. In pairs or small groups, have students work collaboratively to complete the exercise.
2. Elicit answers.

For Option 1 or 2

1. In pairs or small groups, have students discuss:
   - *Why are the inappropriate paraphrases not as good?*
2. Elicit answers. (Answer: See answer key)

How to paraphrase

Option 1

1. Have students read the explanation on the five steps of paraphrasing on page 75.
2. In pairs or small groups, books closed, have students summarize to each other what they read.
3. Elicit:
   - *What are the five steps for paraphrasing?* (Answer: See page 75)
4. Emphasize:
   - *Step 3 advises to not look at the original text. This is to make sure that the writer does not copy the original too closely.*

Option 2

1. Have students read the explanation on the five steps of paraphrasing on page 75.
2. Then write the sample sentence from Step 1 on the board:
   Only 9% of the students who work part-time earn sufficient income to support themselves.
3. Next, write slashes between the sections of information that can be rearranged:
   Only 9% / of the students who work part-time / earn sufficient income to support themselves.
4. Then underline the shared language:
   Only 9% / of the students who work part-time / earn sufficient income to support themselves.
5. Then write alternatives for the key vocabulary.
   work part-time = have part-time jobs
   earn sufficient income = make enough money
   support themselves = earn a living
6. Then write the sample paraphrase from Step 3:
   Of all the students who have part-time jobs, 9% make enough money to earn a living.
7. Then write the sample paraphrase from Step 5:
   Of all the students who work part-time jobs, only 9% make enough money to earn a living.
8. Have students re-read the points in Step 4.
9. Then elicit:
   - *Why was "have" changed to "work"?* (Answer: **To not have more than three words in a row from the original**)
   - *Why was "only" added before 9%?* (Answer: **The meaning is slight different from the original without "only"**)

Exercise 2

Option 1

1. Have students do the exercise individually.
2. Then in pairs or small groups, have students compare their answers.

3. Elicit answers.

Option 2

1. In pairs or small groups, have students work collaboratively to complete the exercise.
2. Elicit answers.

After Option 1 or 2

Another way to check answers:
1. For each item, have a few students come up to the board to write their paraphrases.
2. Compare similarities and differences.

Option 3

Have everyone in the class do this exercise at the same pace by keeping time through each step:
1. Have students work individually or in pairs.
2. Start with sentence 1.
   - Have students follow Step 1 (20 seconds)
   - Then have students follow Step 2 (30 seconds)
   - In pairs, have students compare notes.
   - Then have students cover the original sentence with their hand, and follow Step 3 (60 seconds)
   - In pairs, have students compare what they wrote.
   - Then have students follow Step 4 (40 seconds)
   - Then have students follow Step 5 (30 seconds)
   - In pairs, have students compare what they wrote.

Note: Adjust these recommended times to suit the level of your class.

3. When done, for each item, have a few students come up to the board to write their paraphrases.
4. Compare similarities and differences.
5. Repeat the process for each of the remaining sentences.

Section 3 **Summarizing**

Option 1

1. Have students read the explanation and example summary.
2. Write the following on the board:
   A summary should contain the _____ from the original.

   It should use _____ vocabulary and structure from the original.

   The summary should be _____ than the original.
3. In pairs, have students discuss how to complete these rules.
4. Elicit answers. (Answers: First rule = **main idea**, second rule = **different**, third rule = **shorter**)

Option 2

1. Have students read the explanation on page 76 only.

2. Quickly elicit: *What are the rules for writing a summary?*
(Answer)
   - **It should contain the main idea from the original.**
   - **It should use different vocabulary and structure from the original.**
   - **It should be shorter than the original.**

Option 3

1. Have students read the sample paragraph on page 76.
2. Then have students read the sample summaries at the top of page 77 but cover the explanation below the summaries with their hand or a piece of paper.
3. In pairs, have students discuss:
   - *What is the problem with summaries a and b?*
4. Elicit answers. (Answer: See explanation on page 77)

Exercise 3

Option 1

1. Have students do the exercise individually.
2. Then in pairs or small groups, have students compare their answers.
3. Elicit answers.

Option 2

1. In pairs or small groups, have students work collaboratively to complete the exercise.
2. Elicit answers.

For Option 1 or 2

1. In pairs or small groups, have students discuss:
   - *Why are the summaries you didn't choose not as good?*
2. Elicit answers. (Answer: See answer key)

Option 3

Before deciding on their answer, have students:
1. Underline the key vocabulary in each summary and check to see if it is the same as the vocabulary used in the original passage.
2. Draw slashes between the groups of ideas in each summary so they can see if the structure has changed from the original or not, e.g.:
Because of its <u>effectiveness</u>, <u>low cost</u>, and <u>cultural value</u>, / <u>many people in the world</u> / <u>prefer traditional medicine</u> to <u>modern medicine</u>.

How to summarize
Option 1

1. Have students read the explanation on the six steps of summarizing on pages 78 and 79.
2. In pairs or small groups, books closed, have students summarize to each other what they read.

3. Elicit:
   - *What are the six steps for summarizing?*
   (Answer: See pages 78 and 79)
4. Emphasize:
   - *The process for summarizing is similar to the process for paraphrasing, but it includes the extra element of deciding what the key information in the original source is (Step 2).*

Option 2

1. Have students compare the sample summary in Step 4 with the sample summary in Step 6.
2. Elicit:
   - *Why were the words "worldwide" and "serious" added to the Step 6 summary?*
   (Answer: **The two words help make the summary more accurately reflect the key points from the original.**)

Option 3

To help students identify key points:
1. Have students look at the sample paragraph on page 78.
2. Elicit:
   - *Why are the two highlighted areas considered key points?*
   (Answer: **Because the key points are general ideas which are being supported by more specific details.**)
3. Emphasize:
   - *Distinguishing key points from details can be difficult. This often causes students to write summaries that are too long or too short.*
   - *Most students tend to write summaries that are too long. Therefore, if unsure whether to include particular information in the summary or not, it is usually better to leave it out.*
   - *Summaries to be included in academic essays should be no more than one or two sentences.*

Exercise 4

Option 1

1. Have students do the exercise individually.
2. Then in pairs or small groups, have students compare their answers.
3. Elicit answers.

Option 2

1. In pairs or small groups, have students work collaboratively to complete the exercise.
2. Elicit answers.

Option 3

1. In pairs or small groups, for each passage, have students discuss:
   - *What are the key points?*
   Advise students to choose no more than two or three parts, if possible.
2. Elicit answers. (Answer: See sample summary in the answer key; key points mentioned)

3. Then have students discuss:
   - *What is the shared language?*
4. Elicit answers. (Answer: See sample summary in the answer key, words repeated from original)
5. Then have students discuss:
   - *What are alternative ways to write what is not shared language?*
6. Finally, have students individually write a summary of each passage.
7. Elicit answers. (Answer: See sample summary in the answer key)

After Option 1, 2, or 3

Another way to check answers:
1. For each item, have a few students come up to the board to write their summaries.
2. Compare similarities and differences.

Review questions

Option 1

Elicit answers to the Review questions on page 80.

Option 2

1. Have students in pairs or small groups ask each other the questions on page 80.
2. Elicit answers when done.

UNIT 3

Part 2
Citing the sources of information

Section 1 — Introduction

Option 1

1. Have students read pages 81 and 82.

2. In pairs or small groups, books closed, have students summarize to each other what they read.

3. Elicit:
   - *What are four purposes of citation?* (Answer)
     - **To show that the information is not the writer's own**
     - **To show where information comes from**
     - **To allow readers to find this information for themselves**
     - **To avoid plagiarism**
   - *What is common knowledge?* (Answer: **Widely known facts, widely reported events**)
   - *What are the two parts of citation?* (Answer: **In-text citation and a Works Cited list**)

Option 2

Emphasize the importance of avoiding plagiarism:
1. Elicit:
   - *What is plagiarism?*
   - *How does citation help prevent plagiarism?*

2. Emphasize:
   - *Plagiarism may be viewed much more negatively in an English-speaking environment than in the student's current environment.*
   - *At some universities, the penalty for plagiarism is expulsion from school.*

Option 3

Focus on common knowledge:
1. Elicit:
   - *What are some other widely known facts?* (Possible answers)
     - **The population of Japan is shrinking.**
     - **Earth has one moon.**
   - *What were some other widely reported events?* (Possible answers)
     - **John F. Kennedy was assassinated in 1963.**
     - **In 2011, several Middle Eastern countries saw regime change during what is known as the "Arab Spring."**

2. Emphasize:
   - *Citation is necessary for information which may not be known to most people.*
   - *Citation is also necessary for information that is specific to particular sources (i.e., not widely reported).*
   - *If unsure whether or not information is common knowledge, cite it.*

Section 2 — Making in-text citation (MLA format)

There is a lot of information in this section, so it can be divided into steps.

Step 1

1. Have students read the top of page 83 until the end of the three fundamental rules of in-text citation.

2. In pairs or small groups, books closed, have students summarize to each other what they read.

3. Elicit:
   - *What is the purpose of in-text citation?* (Answer: **To allow the reader to easily find the source in the Works Cited list**)
   - *What are the three fundamental rules of in-text citation?* (Answer: See the three points at the top of page 83)

4. Emphasize:
   - *Students need to use names, page numbers, and possibly titles of sources in in-text citation.*
   - *In-text citation should include enough information so readers can find complete details in the Works Cited list without disrupting the flow of the writing.*

Step 2

1. Have students read parts 1 to 3 on pages 83 and 84.

2. In pairs or small groups, books closed, have students summarize to each other what they read.

3. Elicit:
   - *What is one format when citing if you have the author's name and page number?* (Answer: **Format a or b in the middle of page 83**)
   - *What is another format when citing if you have the author's name and page number?* (Answer: **Format a or b in the middle of page 83**)
   - *What is the format when citing if you have the author's name but no page number?* (Answer: **Format 2 at the bottom of page 83**)
   - *What is the format when citing if you do not have the author's name?* (Answer: **Format 3 at the top of page 84**)

Step 3

1. Have students read part 4 on page 84.

2. In pairs or small groups, books closed, have students summarize to each other what they read.

3. Elicit:
   - *What is "secondary source" information?* (Answer: **Information in a source which is cited as coming from another source**)
   - *Which source should be included in the sentence?* (Answer: **The original source**)
   - *What should be in parenthesis at the end of the sentence?* (Answer: **qtd. in + secondary source + page number**)

Step 4

1. Have students read the information in part 5 on page 85.
2. In pairs or small groups, books closed, have students summarize to each other what they read.
3. Elicit:
   - *What are some common reporting words?* (Answer: See top of page 85)
4. Emphasize:
   - *The reporting words at the top of page 85 are not an exhaustive list.*
   - *It is important to use a variety of reporting words when citing outside sources.*

Exercise 1

Option 1

1. Have students do the exercise individually.
2. Emphasize:
   - *Rewrite the sentences including appropriate in-text citation.*
   - *Follow the guidelines from 1 to 5 in Section 2 on pages 83–85.*
3. Then in pairs or small groups, have students compare their answers.
4. Elicit answers.

Option 2

1. In pairs or small groups, have students work collaboratively to complete the exercise.
2. Emphasize:
   - *Rewrite the sentences including appropriate in-text citation.*
   - *Follow the guidelines from 1 to 5 in Section 2.*
3. Elicit answers.

After Option 1 or 2

Another way to check answers:
1. For each item, have a few students come up to the board to write their in-text citation.
2. Compare similarities and differences.

Section 3   Making a Works Cited list (MLA Format)

Step 1

1. Have students read the paragraph at the top of page 87.
2. In pairs or small groups, books closed, have students summarize to each other what they read.

3. Elicit:
   - *What is the order of the Works Cited list?* (Answer: **Alphabetical**)
   - *Where is the Works Cited list located?* (Answer: **On a separate page at the end of the essay**)

Step 2

1. Have students read the five examples of how to cite the different sources.
2. Emphasize:
   - *Do not memorize this information.*
   - *Simply refer to it as needed and follow the format accurately.*

Step 3

1. Have students read the information in the top half of page 88.
2. In pairs or small groups, books closed, have students summarize to each other what they read.
3. Elicit:
   - *What are the Works Cited rules when you have two or more authors?* (Answer: **List names in order they appear on title page; reverse only the first author's name.**)
   - *What are the Works Cited rules when the author's name is not given?* (Answer: **Begin with the title.**)
   - *What are the Works Cited rules when the source is written by a group?* (Answer: **Begin with the name of the group.**)

Step 4

1. Have students look at the three example body paragraphs on pages 88 and 89. (Note: The three paragraphs are from the example essay in Unit 4 Part 1 on page 95.)
2. Have students notice:
   - *The arrows showing the relationship between in-text citation and the Works Cited list.*
   - *The information used in the in-text citation – when an author's name is used, when a source title is used, and when page numbers are included.*

Exercise 2

Option 1

1. Have students do the exercise individually.
2. Explain:
   - *The Works Cited list is accurate.*
   - *Focus on problems with in-text citation in the sentences.*
3. Then in pairs or small groups, have students compare their answers.
4. Elicit answers.

Option 2

1. In pairs or small groups, have students work collaboratively to complete the exercise.

2. Explain:
   • *The Works Cited list is accurate.*
   • *Focus on problems with in-text citation in the sentences.*
3. Elicit answers.

Exercise 3

Option 1

1. Have students do the exercise individually.
2. Advise:
   • *Pay attention to the use of periods and spaces between different parts of the entry.*
3. Then in pairs or small groups, have students compare their answers.
4. Elicit answers.

Option 2

1. In pairs or small groups, have students work collaboratively to complete the exercise.
2. Have each pair/group choose one writer.
3. Other students should look at the rules on page 87 and the sources on pages 85 and 86, and tell the writer what to write.
4. Advise:
   • *Pay attention to the use of periods and spaces between different parts of the entry.*
5. Elicit answers.

After Option 1 or 2

Another way to check answers:
1. Have five students come up to different parts of the board. Have each write a different Works Cited entry.
2. Go to each entry and elicit from students:
   • *Are there any errors?*
   • *(if yes) How do you correct it?*

Review questions

Option 1

Elicit answers to the Review questions on page 90.

Option 2

1. Have students in pairs or small groups ask each other the questions on page 90.
2. Elicit answers when done.

UNIT 4

Part 1
Developing and organizing a research essay

Option 1

1. To introduce the topic of research, write the following sentence on the board:
   Polar bears will be extinct by the year 2050 if more is not done to protect them.

2. Elicit:
   - *What do you think of this statement? Do you believe it?*

3. Then add the words "A study from the California Marine Studies Institute claims that" in front of the sentence so it looks like this:
   A study from the California Marine Studies Institute claims that polar bears will be extinct by 2050 if more is not done to protect them.

4. Elicit:
   - *Now what do you think of this statement? Do you believe it?*

5. Emphasize:
   - *Research adds credibility to a writer's argument.*
   - *Without research, readers are less likely to believe what they read in an essay.*

Option 2

1. Have students read page 92.

2. In pairs or small groups, books closed, have students summarize to each other what they read.

3. Elicit:
   - *What is the difference between a research essay and the essay type you studied in Unit 2?* (Answer: **A research essay contains information from outside sources. It is not just your personal opinions.**)
   - *What will readers likely think of an essay which does not have research?* (Answer: **That the essay is a subjective personal opinion and not convincing**)

4. Emphasize:
   - *A research essay is more academic because it includes the opinions of experts on the topic of the essay.*
   - *Before writing a research essay, do research before taking a position on the topic. See what the different positions and arguments are, then decide which are the most convincing. This will make it easier when writing the essay and supporting it effectively.*
   - *Use the in-text citation techniques in Unit 3 when writing a research essay.*

Section 2 The structure of a research essay

Option 1

1. Have students read pages 93 and 94.

2. In pairs or small groups, books closed, have students summarize to each other what they read.

3. Elicit:
   - *What are the three major parts of a research essay?* (Answer: **introductory paragraph, body paragraphs, concluding paragraph**
   - *What are the two parts of the introductory paragraph?* (Answer: **building sentences and thesis**)
   - *What are the three parts of a body paragraph?* (Answer: **topic sentence, supporting sentences, concluding sentence**)
   - *What are the three parts of the concluding paragraph?* (Answer: **restatement of thesis, summary of body paragraphs, final thought**)

4. As each answer is given correctly, write it on the board and follow up with the question:
   - *What is the function of that part?* (Answers: See page 94)

Option 2

To review the essay structure from Unit 2:
1. Do not have students read pages 93 and 94 yet.

2. Write the following on the board:

Essay

Paragraph 1: _____

1.

2.

Paragraphs 2, 3, and 4: _____

1.

2.

3.

Paragraph 5: _____

1.

2.

3.

3. In pairs or small groups, have students discuss:
   - *What information belongs in each blank space?*

4. Elicit answers and write them in the appropriate spaces.

5. Then have students open the textbook to page 94 and check their answers.

6. Explain:
   - *A research essay has the same elements, in the same order, as the essay type presented in Unit 2.*

Exercise 1

Option 1

1. Have students do part 1 of the exercise individually.

2. Instruct:
   - *Draw a line from a particular sentence or section to the closest margin (top, bottom, left, or right).*
   - *Next to each line, write the name of that part in the margin.*

3. Then in pairs or small groups, have students compare their answers.

4. Elicit answers.

5. Then have students do part 2 in pairs or small groups without looking back at the essay.

Option 2

1. Without doing anything from Exercise 1 yet, simply have students read the essay.

2. Then in pairs or small groups, books closed, have students summarize to each other what they read.

3. Then have the pairs/groups do part 1 of the exercise.

Option 3

1. Micro-analyze the essay. Have students read the first paragraph.

2. Then, books closed, have students summarize what they read with a partner.

3. Elicit answers to the question:
   - *What information is in the paragraph?*

4. Repeat the process for each of the rest of the paragraphs.

Section 3 — Beginning a research essay

Option 1

1. Have students read all the information on page 97.

2. Elicit:
   - *What should you do before writing an essay?* (Answer: **Make a list of the different views on the topic**)
   - *What should you make sure you include on this list?* (Answer: **Source information – author's name, title of publication, or article name plus the page number**)

3. Emphasize:
   - *Writers often waste time trying to find where certain information they have researched came from because they did not keep a record of it.*

- *Therefore, note the source next to the information listed to save time when writing the essay later.*
- *For some sources, there is no page number, so none can be included. Other sources may not identify the author, so the title should be used instead.*

Option 2

1. Have students look at the whaling arguments in the table on page 97.

2. In pairs or small groups, have students discuss:
   - *Which ideas do you agree with?*

3. Then have students discuss:
   - *What is your position on this topic?*
   - *What are the three strongest arguments supporting your position?*

4. Elicit answers from a few students.

5. Emphasize:
   - *Although the textbook teaches only five-paragraph essay structures, many essays are longer.*
   - *However, it is important for writers to decide and present only the most important supporting arguments.*
   - *It is possible to present too much information that could distract readers.*

Exercise 2

Option 1

1. In pairs or small groups, have students work collaboratively to complete the exercise.

2. Have each pair/group choose one issue.

3. Have each pair/group choose one writer.

4. All of the students should give ideas for both positions on the issue for the writer to note down.

5. Remind students:
   - *After listing the arguments, take a position.*
   - *Decide the two or three arguments which best support your position.*

6. To elicit answers, first draw a T-table on the board and label the two columns "for" and "against," like this:

For	Against

7. Select a few individual students and ask:
   - *Which issue did you choose?*

8. Write the topic above the table.

9. Then ask:
   - *What arguments did you come up with?*

10. Write the arguments on the table on the appropriate side.

11. Then ask:
    - *What is your position on the issue?*
    - *What are the strongest arguments supporting your position?*

12. Then ask the rest of the class:
    - *Did anyone else choose the same topic?*
13. If yes, then ask:
    - *Are there any other arguments which could be added to this table?*
14. Write down any additional arguments students give.
15. Then ask any of the students who gave additional arguments:
    - *What is your position on the issue?*
    - *What are the strongest arguments supporting your position?*
16. Next select another student from a different pair/group who did a different topic and repeat the process from step 7 above with a new T-table.

Option 2

1. Have students do the exercise individually.
2. Then in pairs or small groups, have students compare their answers.
3. Elicit answers as described in step 6 from Option 1.

Section 4 — Writing a thesis statement for a research essay

Option 1

To review thesis statements presented in Unit 2:
1. Elicit:
    - *What is the most important sentence in an essay?* (Answer: **the thesis statement**)
    - *What is the purpose of the thesis statement?* (Answer: **tells the reader the purpose and contents of the essay**)
    - *What are the three parts of a thesis statement?* (Answer: **topic, writer's position, main ideas**)
2. Emphasize:
    - *A thesis statement in a research essay has the same parts and purpose as the thesis statement from Unit 2.*
    - *However, for research essays, the term "position" is used instead of "opinion," which was used in Unit 2. This is to emphasize that in a research essay, a writer is expected to take a position on an issue and use cited information to help support that position.*
3. Have students read the explanation on page 98.

Option 2

To focus on the idea of switching the position of the writer's position and main ideas:
1. Write the following on the board:
   Clearly, the benefits of tourism outweigh the costs because tourism provides employment for local people, encourages the preservation of native culture, and helps to improve infrastructure.
2. Ask students to identify:
    - *the topic* (Answer: **The benefits of tourism**)
    - *the position* (Answer: **The benefits of tourism outweigh the costs.**)

- *the main ideas* (Answers: **provides employment, encourages preservation of local culture, improves infrastructure**)
3. Then ask students to write a version of this thesis with the main ideas first and the position second.
4. Elicit answers from a few students.

   (Possible answer: **Clearly, because tourism provides employment for local people, encourages the preservation of native culture, and helps to improve infrastructure, the benefits of tourism outweigh the costs.**)

Exercise 3

Option 1

1. Have students do the exercise individually.
2. Then in pairs or small groups, have students compare their answers.
3. Elicit answers.

Option 2

1. In pairs or small groups, have students work collaboratively to complete the exercise.
2. Elicit answers.

After Option 1 or 2

Another way to check answers:
1. Select students to come up to the board and write their thesis statements.
2. Compare similarities and differences.

Section 5 — Writing topic sentences for a research essay

Option 1

1. Have students read the explanation on page 100.
2. Elicit:
    - *What are the three parts of the topic sentence of a body paragraph?* (Answer: **transitional expression, position from thesis, one of the main ideas from the thesis**)

Option 2

Before reading page 100, review the information about topic sentences presented in Unit 2 (much of the information is similar):
1. In pairs or small groups, have students discuss:
   What are the three parts of the topic sentence of a body paragraph? (Answer: **transitional expression, opinion from thesis, one of the main ideas from the thesis**)
2. Then have students read page 100 to check their answers.

Exercise 4

Option 1

1. Have students do the exercise individually.

2. Then in pairs or small groups, have students compare their answers.

3. Elicit answers.

Option 2

1. In pairs or small groups, have students work collaboratively to complete the exercise.

2. Elicit answers.

After Option 1 or 2

Another way to check answers:

1. For each item, have a few students come up to the board to write their three topic sentences.

2. Compare similarities and differences.

Section 6 Making an outline for a research essay

1. To review the points presented in Unit 2 on essay outlines, elicit:
   - *What should you do before writing an essay?* (Answer: **make an outline**)
   - *Why is this step necessary?* (Answer)
     - **Before writing, helps the writer form ideas and structure them logically.**
     - **While writing, gives guidance by helping the writer stay focused on supporting the thesis.**
   - *What are the four elements in an essay outline?* (Answer: **topic, thesis, topic sentences, supporting points**)
   - *When you make an essay outline, which of the following elements must be a complete sentence?*
     Topic
     Thesis
     Topic sentences
     Supporting points
     (Answer: **Everything except the supporting points**)

2. Have students read the explanation on page 102.

   Note: The textbook lists five elements to be included in an essay outline, but the third point ["the supporting argument (main idea) of each body paragraph"] is not necessary – it should be included as the controlling idea of the topic sentence in the body paragraph.

Exercise 5

Option 1

1. Have students do the exercise individually.

2. Then in pairs or small groups, have students compare their answers.

3. Elicit answers.

Option 2

1. In pairs or small groups, have students try to recall the missing supporting points without looking back at the essay on page 95.

2. Elicit answers.

Exercise 6

Option 1

1. Have students do the exercise individually.

2. When done, in pairs or small groups, have students compare their outlines.

Option 2

1. In the same pairs or small groups from Exercise 2, have students work collaboratively to complete the exercise.

2. When done, have the student pairs/groups show their outline to another pair/group.

For Option 1 or 2

1. To elicit answers select a few students and have them read their outline.

2. Give comments on the thesis statement and topic sentences based on:
   - Structure
   - Word choice
   - Grammar

Review questions

Option 1

Elicit answers to the Review questions on page 105.

Option 2

1. Have students in pairs or small groups ask each other the questions on page 105.

2. Elicit answers when done.

UNIT 4

Part 2
Supporting arguments

Section 1 | Supporting arguments with outside sources

Option 1

To focus on types of outside sources:
1. Elicit:
   - *What types of outside source are commonly researched when writing an academic essay?* (Possible answers: **books, academic journals, magazines, newspapers, internet**)

Option 2

1. Have students read page 106.
2. Elicit:
   - *What are four types of information that can support an argument?* (Answer: **facts, anecdotes, statistics, experts' opinions**)

Section 2 | Organizing supporting sentences

1. Have students read the explanations and examples on pages 107 and 108.
2. Elicit:
   - *What should you consider when choosing information to use in your essay?* (Answer: **Is the information relevant, specific, and is it an example, statistic, or expert's opinion which supports your argument?**)
3. Emphasize:
   - *When choosing which information to include in an essay, ask yourself:*
     - *Does the information show in detail how the supporting point is true?*
   - *In the end, there should be a logical relationship between all of the information in the essay:*
     - *Information from outside sources should show how the supporting point is true.*
     - *The supporting points should show how the controlling idea in the topic sentence is true.*
     - *All of the controlling ideas on the topic should show how the thesis is true.*

Exercise 1

Option 1

1. Have students do the exercise individually.
2. For part 2, have students draw an arrow from the information to the idea that it supports.
3. Then in pairs or small groups, have students compare their answers.
4. Elicit answers.

Option 2

1. In pairs or small groups, have students work collaboratively to complete the exercise.
2. For part 2, have students draw an arrow from the information to the idea that it supports.
3. Elicit answers.

Exercise 2

Option 1

1. Have students do the exercise individually.
2. Then in pairs or small groups, have students discuss:
   - *Which is the correct answer? Why?*
   - *Why are the other answers less effective?*
3. Elicit answers.

Option 2

1. In pairs or small groups, have students work collaboratively to complete the exercise by discussing:
   - *Which is the correct answer? Why?*
   - *Why are the other answers less effective?*
2. Elicit answers.

Section 3 | Presenting information from outside sources

Option 1

Review the information on paraphrasing and summarizing from Unit 3:
1. Elicit:
   - *What are the rules for paraphrasing?* (Answer)
     - **Write in your own words.**
     - **Keep the same details as the original.**
     - **Do not change ideas from the original.**
     - **Do not remove or add new ideas.**
   - *What are the rules for writing a summary?* (Answer)
     - **It should contain the main idea from the original.**
     - **It should use different vocabulary and structure from the original.**
     - **It should be shorter than the original.**

Option 2

1. Have students read the table on page 109.
2. In pairs or small groups, books closed, have students discuss:
   - *What are the similarities and differences between paraphrasing, summarizing, and quoting?*

3. As the students are discussing, draw the table on page 109 on the board, but only include the titles "Paraphrasing," "Summarizing," and "Quotation" on the top, and the three questions on the left side.

4. Elicit answers and fill in the table.

5. Have students look again at the table on page 109 to check what is missing.

Option 3

To focus on quotation (not covered previously in the book):

1. Have students read the information under the title "Quoting" on pages 109 and 110.

2. In pairs or small groups, books closed, have students summarize to each other what they read.

3. Elicit:
   - *What are the rules for using a quotation in an essay?*
     (Answer)
     - **Use quotation marks.**
     - **Use the exact same words as the original.**
     - **Do not overuse quotations.**
   - *When should you use a quotation in an essay?*
     (Answer: **When the original writing is impressive and strongly supports your argument**)

4. Emphasize:
   - *On page 110, pay attention to how the author's name is included in the sentence (not in parentheses) and how the page number is also included at the end. Quoting requires the same elements of in-text citation as paraphrasing and summarizing.*
   - *Avoid quoting too much for a couple of reasons:*
     - *Directly copying words, while easy, is not as valuable a skill as paraphrasing and summarizing, because paraphrasing and summarizing shows that you understand the original source and can express it in your own words. Quoting only shows that you have read the original source.*
     - *Quoting too much may make the essay seem like other people's writing, not your own. In other words, readers may think you do not have any of your own ideas on the topic.*

Exercise 3

Before doing Option 1 or 2

Emphasize that there are three steps to this exercise:

1. *Read the five sources and decide which one is the most appropriate for each statement. Refer to page 107 for criteria on choosing information to include in an essay.*

2. *Decide the most appropriate way of presenting the information. Refer to the table on page 109 for criteria on deciding this.*

3. *Write the sentences. For structuring a cited paraphrase or summary, refer to pages 83–85. For structuring a quotation, refer to the top of page 110.*

Option 1

1. Have students do the exercise individually.

2. Then in pairs or small groups, have students compare their answers.

3. Elicit answers.

Option 2

1. In pairs or small groups, have students work collaboratively to complete the exercise.

2. Elicit answers.

Option 3

1. For the information from outside sources not selected, have students (individually, in pairs, or in small groups) write a statement which could support that information.
   (Possible answers)
   - **Source a: It seems governments should make efforts to try to promote tourism in their countries.**
   - **Source c: There is the potential that many pieces of history will be lost forever.**
   - **Source d: Hawaii seems to be a leader in protecting their ecosystem.**

2. Elicit answers.

Review questions

Option 1

Elicit answers to the Review questions on page 111.

Option 2

1. Have students in pairs or small groups ask each other the questions on page 111.

2. Elicit answers when done.

Section 1 — Making accurate generalizations

Option 1

1. Have students read page 112.

2. In pairs or small groups, books closed, have students summarize to each other what they read.

3. Elicit:
   - *What is an overgeneralization?*
     (Answer: **Claiming something is true in all cases, when in reality it is not**)
   - *Why do overgeneralizations make an essay weaker?*
     (Answer: **They will weaken an argument and may make the reader doubt the claim, and even the credibility of the writer.**)

4. Have students read the rest of the section on pages 113 and 114.

5. In pairs or small groups, books closed, have students summarize to each other what they read.

6. Elicit:
   - *What are three structures that can be used to make accurate generalizations?* (Answer: **expressions of quantity, adverbs of frequency and certain modal auxiliaries/verbs, e.g., "may," "might," "tend to," "likely"**)

Option 2

(Before doing option 1)

1. Write the first example sentence on page 112 on the board:
   People should be allowed to shoot tigers that wander into villages because these tigers attack farm animals and villagers.

2. In pairs, have students look at the statement and discuss:
   - *What is wrong with this sentence?*

3. Elicit answers.
   (Answer: **The sentence makes an overgeneralization about tigers. It's likely not 100% true.**)

Note:

1. If students are having trouble answering the question, underline the words "these tigers attack farm animals and villagers."

2. Then elicit:
   - *Does the sentence mean that this action happens sometimes, often, usually, or all the time?*

Option 3

(Before doing Option 1)

1. Write the following sentences on the board:
   In 50 years, the average lifespan of humans will be over 100 years old.
   The most important invention of the 20th century is the personal computer.
   Americans are obese.

2. In pairs or small groups, have students discuss:
   - *Are these sentences acceptable?*

3. Elicit answers. (Answer: **These sentences are making overgeneralizations. In other words, they make claims that are likely not 100% true, and so can easily be doubted.**)

4. Emphasize:
   - *The last sentence about Americans is also potentially offensive, since it is a stereotype.*
   - *Be especially careful not to overgeneralize particular nationalities.*

5. In pairs or small groups, have students discuss:
   - *How do you fix these sentences?*

6. Elicit answers and fix the sentences on the board as suggestions are given.
   (Possible answers)
   - In 50 years, the average lifespan of humans will <u>possibly</u> be over 100 years old.
   - <u>A number of researchers claim that</u> in 50 years, the average lifespan of humans will be over 100 years old.
   - <u>One of</u> the most important inventions of the 20th century is the personal computer.
   - <u>Many people believe that</u> the most important invention of the 20th century is the personal computer.
   - <u>Many</u> Americans are obese.
   - <u>Studies show that most</u> Americans are obese. There are a lot of obese people, but the percentage is less than a third of total population. That means "most" is not accurate. Change to "a large number" or "a third of"?

7. Emphasize:
   - *Overgeneralization is probably the biggest and simplest mistake that writers can make.*
   - *Students may be tempted to make generalizations because they seem like strong or persuasive statements, but in fact the opposite is true – they are weak because they are ill-informed and inaccurate.*
   - *Rarely is a claim 100% true. If a claim is likely not 100% true, then words need to be changed or added to make the claim seem more believable.*
   - *The shaded boxes on pages 113 and 114 contain vocabulary which helps make a claim seem more accurate.*

Option 1

1. Have students do the exercise individually.
2. Then in pairs or small groups, have students compare their answers.
3. Elicit answers.

Option 2

1. In pairs or small groups, have students work collaboratively to complete the exercise.
2. Elicit answers.

For Option 1 or 2

Before students start, emphasize:
- *Use a range of vocabulary in this exercise, particularly words that you do not often use in your own writing.*
- *This exercise involves personal opinions, so how you change each sentence depends on how you feel about the issue.*

Section 2   Editing a research essay

Option 1

If students have studied Unit 2 Part 3 ("Editing an essay"), then do a quick review:
1. In pairs or small groups, have students discuss:
   - *How many stages of editing are there and what should you check in each stage?*
2. Elicit answers.
   (Answer: **Editing should be done in two stages – the first stage is for content and organization and the second stage is for grammar and style.**)
3. Then have students read the explanation and look at the checklist on page 115.
4. In pairs or small groups, books open, have students discuss:
   - *How is this checklist different from the checklist on page 69?*
5. Elicit answers.
   (Answer)
   The editing checklist on page 115 emphasizes:
   - **whether a position is clear.**
   - **if it is strongly supported by outside sources.**
   - **if citation is done properly.**

Option 2

1. Have students read the explanation and look at the checklist on page 115.
2. Then elicit:
   - *How many times should you read a research essay when editing it?*
   - *What should you check during each reading?*

3. Elicit answers:
   (Answer)
   There should be two readings minimum:
   - **First reading is to check for content and organization.**
   - **Second reading is for citation and grammar and style.**

Option 3

1. Before looking at the textbook, in pairs or small groups, have students discuss:
   - *What do you need to check when editing a research essay?*
2. Elicit answers.
   (Answer: **Content, organization, citation, grammar and style**)
3. Then write on the board:
   Content
   Organization
   Citation
   Grammar and style
4. In pairs or small groups, have students discuss:
   - *What questions should you ask about each when editing?*
5. Elicit answers.
6. Refer students to the Research Essay Editing Checklist on page 115.
7. Emphasize:
   - *The checklist presents the more important things first – checking for content, then organization, then citation, then grammar and style.*
   - *Don't worry too much about grammar. Successfully completing an essay is more about content and organization than grammar.*

Option 1

1. Have students do Step 1 of the exercise individually.
2. When done, in pairs or small groups, have students compare their answers.
3. Elicit answers.
4. Then have students do Step 2 of the exercise individually.
5. When done, in pairs or small groups, have students compare their answers.
6. Elicit answers.

Option 2

1. In pairs or small groups, have students work collaboratively to complete Step 1 of the exercise.
2. Have each pair/group compare their comments with another pair's/group's.
3. Elicit answers.
4. In pairs or small groups, have students work collaboratively to complete Step 2 of the exercise.

5. Have each pair/group compare their edits/comments with another pair's/group's.

6. Elicit answers.

For both Option 1 and 2

Emphasize:
- *This exercise is not just about finding mistakes. It is important to suggest actual ways to make improvements.*
- *Focus on all parts of the essay, as all parts contain mistakes.*
- *Look for positive things as well. Comment on what is successful in the essay.*

Review questions

Option 1

Elicit answers to the Review questions on page 118.

Option 2

1. Have students in pairs or small groups ask each other the questions on page 118.

2. Elicit answers when done.

Answer Key

UNIT 1 PART 1

Exercise 1

p.2

1. Reasons for going to university
2. (Answers)
   1. *"However, in spite of these opportunities, some students cannot find a rewarding job after graduation because of unfavorable economic conditions."*
   2. *"Sometimes students make friends through part-time jobs too."*

   (Explanations)
   1. *"Students cannot find a rewarding job . . . because of unfavorable economic conditions"* refers to a situation after university, so is irrelevant to reasons for going to university.
   2. People can make friends through part-time jobs without going to university, so making friends through part-time jobs cannot be a reason for going to university.

Exercise 2

p. 4

1. **Topic sentence:**

   After graduating from high school, many students go on to university, but their reasons for entering higher education vary.

   Supporting sentences:
   First, many students attend university to study a particular subject in depth. Unlike high schools, which require students to take a wide range of classes, university curriculums allow students to choose a major. In each major, a number of specialized courses are offered, and they are taught by experts in the fields. Moreover, universities have various research facilities that help students learn. Another common reason for going to university is that a college education often leads to a better career in the future. In many countries, people with university degrees tend to find better-paying jobs than those without them. In addition, some universities provide their students with opportunities to acquire practical skills that can be useful in the real world, such as accounting, using computers, and speaking foreign languages. Finally, for some students, making friends and enjoying an active social life can be a sufficient reason to stay in school for another four years. In universities, students have chances to meet people who come from different places with diverse backgrounds. Furthermore, universities have a variety of student organizations where students can meet others with similar interests and spend time with them.

   Concluding sentence:
   To sum up, students go to university for a variety of reasons: to study a particular field, to find a good job, or to make friends.

2. (Answers)
   a) Reasons for going to university vary.
   b) There are three supporting points.
      Supporting point 1: To study a particular subject in depth
      Supporting point 2: To find a better career
      Supporting point 3: To make friends and enjoy an active social life

Exercise 3

p. 7

Answers will vary.

(Example answer for topic 4 "Factors in choosing a university")

Listing:
   Factors in choosing a university
   - major
   - location
   - size
   - student–professor ratio
   - professors and their qualifications
   - library facilities
   - private or public
   - expense (tuition, room and board)
   - scholarships/financial aid
   - after-school entertainment

Mind mapping:
See diagram at the top of the next page.

Free writing:
Maybe the first thing people consider is their major. Unlike high school, where you have to study a variety of subjects, in university, you choose a major and study it in depth, so it is important to think which university offers the major you want to study. Some universities have famous professors to teach certain subjects, so you should think about that too. The next thing is location. Do they want to go to universities in their hometown or do they want to go to different cities? Do they want to go to universities in urban or rural areas? For me, if a university is located in a very rural area, the life outside of school might become very boring . . .

Exercise 4

p. 9

(Answers)

1. b
2. c
3. b

(Explanations)

1. **b** is the best topic sentence because it expresses the topic ("clubs at university") and the controlling idea ("there are three types of clubs at university") clearly. **a** is too general because it says that universities usually have many sports clubs while the controlling idea specifies that there are three types of clubs at university.

Mind map for Exercise 3 on previous page

c contains the topic ("clubs at university"), but it does not contain the controlling idea ("three types of clubs at university").

2. c is the best topic sentence because it expresses the topic ("living in a university dormitory") and the controlling idea ("living in a dormitory has many benefits for university students") clearly. a is too general because it has the topic ("university dormitory"), but it does not have the controlling idea ("many benefits"). b is too specific because it states "free air conditioning" as the only benefit of living in a dormitory while the controlling idea suggests that there are many benefits.

3. b is the best topic sentence because it expresses the topic ("academic writing skills for university students") and the controlling idea ("essential for high grades in university") clearly. a has the topic ("academic writing skills") but is inappropriate because it expresses an idea that is not included in the controlling idea (i.e., "throughout their lives" is not in the controlling idea). c is too specific because it suggests that academic writing skills are necessary for good grades only in literature, whereas the controlling idea suggests that such skills are essential for high grades in university in general.

Exercise 5

p. 12

Answers will vary.

(Example answer for the topic "Factors in choosing a university")

Outline

Topic: Factors in choosing a university

Topic sentence:
When students decide which university to attend, they take various factors into consideration.

Supporting points:
1. If there are well-qualified professors to teach the majors they want
2. Whether the university is in a suitable location
3. Whether they can afford to pay the tuition fees

UNIT 1 PART 2

Exercise 1

p. 14

2. **To prepare for a future career:**
   a) People with university degrees tend to find better-paying jobs
   b) Opportunities to acquire practical skills (accounting, using computers, speaking foreign languages)

3. **To make friends and enjoy an active social life:**
   a) Meet people from different places and with different backgrounds
   b) Join student organizations and meet students with similar interests

Exercise 2

p. 16

1. *First, students whose homes are close enough to school often live with their families.*

   e-g

2. *Second, students who live too far away from school to commute might move into a dormitory.*

   a-d-f

3. *Finally, living alone in an apartment is a popular choice among students who cannot commute to school from their homes but do not like the inconveniences of dormitory life.*

   c-b

Exercise 3

p. 18

Answers will vary.

(Example answers for a paragraph about "Factors in choosing a university")

1. In short, sport teams, art clubs, and study groups are three common types of university clubs.

2. To summarize, the advantages of dormitory life are that it helps students make new friends, develop social skills, and reduce costs.

3. To sum up, academic writing skills are useful for university students because they help students complete course assignments successfully, obtain good grades, and gain an advantage in their future career.

Exercise 4

p. 19

Answers will vary.

(Example answer for a paragraph about "Factors in choosing a university")
To summarize, professors, location, and tuition fees are the factors many students examine when they choose their university.

Exercise 5

p. 20

(Answers)

1. b
2. a
3. c

(Explanations)

1. **b** is the best title because it expresses the topic accurately and succinctly – the reader can easily understand that the paragraph will describe different types of university clubs. **a** is too general because it does not contain the idea of "various types." **c** is too specific, suggesting the reader knows there are only "three types" of clubs even before reading. It is also a direct

question. Questions in titles are possible, but they often need the writing topic included, such as "University Clubs: What Are the Differences?"

2. **a** is the best title because it accurately and succinctly expresses that the positive points ("benefits") will be the topic. **b** is a complete sentence. Titles should be key words that announce the topic succinctly, not complete sentences. **c** is too narrowly focused on only one of the three supporting points ("friendship"), and it contains inappropriate emotional, subjective language ("wonderful").

3. **c** is the best title because it expresses the topic of the writing accurately. **a** is inappropriate because it focuses on only one of the three supporting points ("good grades"). **b** is too general; the word *information* is too vague to express the content of the writing ("benefits of academic writing skills").

UNIT 1 PART 3

Exercise 1

p. 20

1. , so
2. , for
3. , but
4. , or
5. and
6. , but
7. , so
8. or
9. , nor
10. , yet

Exercise 2

p. 25

1. because
2. and
3. As
4. but
5. While
6. so
7. so that
8. Unless

Exercise 3

p. 26

1. Since / As
2. so that

3. while / although

4. Whereas / Although / While

5. as

6. Although / While

7. unless

8. If

Exercise 4

p. 27

Answers will vary.

(Example answers)

1. Although the legal drinking age in many countries is between eighteen and twenty-one, some teenagers drink under age.

2. Because the legal drinking age in many countries is between eighteen and twenty-one, stores are prohibited from selling alcohol to minors.

3. The legal drinking age in many countries is between eighteen and twenty-one, so universities should regulate students' drinking more strictly.

4. Although underage drinking can lead to serious health problems, some teenagers drink under age.

5. Since underage drinking can lead to serious health problems, stores are prohibited from selling alcohol to minors.

6. Some teenagers drink under age, so universities should regulate students' drinking more strictly.

7. As underage drinking can lead to serious health problems, universities should regulate students' drinking more strictly.

Exercise 5

p. 29

1. Therefore, / Thus, / As a result,

2. First, / For instance, / For example, Second, / Moreover, / In addition,

3. In contrast, / On the other hand,

4. Similarly, / Likewise,

5. However,

6. In addition, / Moreover,

Exercise 6

p. 31

1. Correct

2. Sentence fragment

   "For example, getting a job, taking a trip, and learning to drive" is a sentence fragment because it lacks a subject-verb sequence. To correct this error, a subject can be added and word forms can be changed to create the subject-verb sequence. Another way to correct this error is to connect the sentence fragment to the previous sentence.

(Example answers)

- Many students use their vacation time to do something they cannot usually do. <u>For example, they get a job, take a trip, and learn to drive</u>.

- Many students use their vacation time to do something they cannot usually do<u>, such as getting a job, taking a trip, and leaning to drive</u>.

3. Sentence fragment

   "Although working while attending school is sometimes stressful" is a sentence fragment because its subordinate conjunction (although) is not attached to an independent clause. To correct this error, the sentence fragment can be attached to the nearby sentence to create a complete sentence.
   (Example answers)

- By working part-time, students can earn extra money and learn about <u>society, although</u> working while attending school is sometimes stressful.

- <u>Although working while attending school is sometimes stressful,</u> students can earn extra money and learn about society by working part-time.

4. Run-on sentence

   It is a run-on sentence because a comma (,) is incorrectly used to combine two independent clauses. To correct this error, the two clauses can be separated into individual sentences, or a correct conjunction can be used.
   (Example answers)

- One advantage of living alone is that it gives complete freedom to <u>students. Another</u> advantage is that students can become independent.

- One advantage of living alone is that it gives complete freedom to <u>students, and</u> another advantage is that students can become independent.

5. Correct

6. Run-on sentence

   It is a run-on sentence because a comma (,) is incorrectly used to combine two independent clauses. To correct this error, the two clauses can be separated into individual sentences, or a correct conjunction can be used.
   (Example answers)

- Email makes communication faster and <u>cheaper. However,</u> it decreases the opportunities for face-to-face communication.

- Email makes communication faster and <u>cheaper, but</u> it decreases the opportunities for face-to-face communication.

7. Sentence fragment

   "So, many students choose to live with their parents" is a sentence fragment because the conjunction *so* is used with only one clause; it should be used to combine two clauses. To correct this error, the sentence fragment can be attached to the nearby sentence to create a complete

sentence, or transitional expressions such as *therefore* and *as a result* can be used to create two separate sentences.

(Example answers)

- Rent is extremely high in many large <u>cities</u>, <u>so</u> many students choose to live with their parents.
- Rent is extremely high in many large <u>cities</u>. <u>Therefore</u>, many students choose to live with their parents.

8. Correct

UNIT 1 PART 4

Exercise 1

p. 33

1. Paragraph A is more academic.
2.
   - Subjective tone (e.g., use of *I*, use of personal experiences as examples)
   - Irrelevant or unnecessary information (e.g., *"I don't want to work in a restaurant . . ."*)
   - Incomplete sentences (e.g., *"And the customers too."*)
   - Short sentences that could be combined (e.g., *"I work at a restaurant. So I have to talk with my boss and senior staff every day."*)
   - Use of first-person narration (e.g., *"I will write about . . ."*)
   - Talking to the reader directly (e.g., *"you should . . ."*)
   - Use of contractions (e.g., *it's, don't*)
   - Colloquial expressions (e.g., *". . . that kind of stuff"*)
   - Unsophisticated or vague vocabulary (e.g., *stuff, kids*)

Exercise 2

p. 36

1.
First Reading:
Content

1. No, the paragraph can be expanded with more details for the first supporting point about "making new friends."
2. Mostly yes, but there is one irrelevant part (see **Comments** below).

Organization

1. There is a title, but it does not represent the topic accurately because it is not specific enough – it does not include the paragraph's content of "reasons why" students go to university. Capital letters are used correctly (see **Comments** below).

2. Yes to both questions.
3. Mostly yes, but there is one irrelevant detail (see **Comments** below).
4. Yes to both questions.

Second reading:

1. There are some errors (see **Problems with grammar and style** below).
2. Yes.
3. Mostly yes, but there are a few errors (see **Problems with grammar and style** below).

Comments:

1. Strengths:
   The three supporting points and most of the details support the controlling idea effectively.
   The topic sentence is clear.
   The supporting sentences are organized correctly under the three supporting points.
   Transitional expressions are used effectively.
   The concluding sentence is written well.

2. Weaknesses:
   - There is irrelevant information; *". . . but maybe you can't accept some of them"* is irrelevant for two reasons. First, it is unnecessary to state that people will not be able to accept the ideas of some other people they meet – it is not connected to the idea of making friends. Second, it is illogical because if you cannot accept someone's ideas, you will not become friends with them; therefore, this detail is not related to the supporting point. The writer could improve this in two ways. First, the writer could add more information about "ideas and a sense of values," for example, *". . . New friends will give them different ideas and new sense of values. This will broaden students' range of knowledge about the world and help them to develop their individual opinions."* Second, the writer could add details of how students can make friends at university, for example, *". . . New friends will give them different sense of values. It is easy to make friends at university because students can meet many people in the same age group who are all going through a similar experience – university education."*
   - The title is too general. It should be "Reasons for Going to University."

2.
Problems with grammar and style:
Grammar

- Incorrect use of coordinating conjunctions:
  "There are many special courses and professors who have a lot of knowledge. <u>So</u> you can learn your major deeply."
- *"<u>And</u> people who graduate from university usually get better job than people who don't graduate from university."*

Coordinating conjunctions should be used to combine two independent clauses, not to start a sentence. At the start of a sentence, transitional expressions should be used (see Unit 1 Part 3, pages 22 and 28).

- Unnecessary comma before the subordinating conjunction *because*:
  "Finally, students go to <u>university, because</u> they can get a better job in the future."

A subordinate clause does not require a comma before the subordinating conjunction if the clause is placed after the independent clause (see Unit 1 Part 3, pages 24–25).

- Use of contractions:
  "And people who graduate from university usually get better job than people who <u>don't</u> graduate from university."

Contractions should not be used in academic essays as they make the tone of writing less formal (see Unit 1 Part 3, page 32).

Style

- Use of *you*:
  "In high school, <u>you</u> had to study many different subjects. However, in university, <u>you</u> can choose a major and study it deeply."

  "There are many special courses and professors who have a lot of knowledge. So <u>you</u> can learn <u>your</u> major deeply."

Using second-person pronouns (*you, your*) in academic essays can degrade the tone of writing. The writer should use more appropriate pronouns such as *they* (see Unit 2 Part 3, page 67).

Corrected draft

The following corrected draft only reflects the editing checklist, so some minor grammar errors remain. In the following, <u>underlines</u> indicate corrected parts and <u>double underlines</u> indicate added parts.

Reasons for Going to University

There are several reasons why students go to university. First, students go to university to make new friends. New friends will give them different ideas and new sense of value. <u>This will broaden students' range of knowledge about the world and help them to develop their individual opinions.</u> It is easy to make friends at university because students can meet many people in the same age group who are all going through a similar experience. Another reason for going to university is to study a subject <u>students</u> are interested in more deeply. In high school, <u>students</u> had to study many different subjects. However, in university, <u>they</u> can choose a major and study it deeply. There are many special courses and professors who have a lot of knowledge<u>, so</u> <u>students</u> can learn <u>their</u> major deeply. Finally, students go to <u>university because</u> they can get a better job in the future. They can learn practical skills which are useful for some jobs through classes and internship program. <u>Moreover,</u> people who graduate from university usually get better job than people who <u>do not</u> graduate from university. To sum up, students go to university to make friends, to study subject they are interested in, and to have a good job in the future.

UNIT 2 PART 1

Exercise 1

p. 41

1. Introductory paragraph = the first paragraph
   Body paragraphs = the second, third, and fourth paragraphs
   Concluding paragraph = the fifth paragraph

2.

Introductory paragraph

- **Building sentences:**
  At one point or another in their high school lives, students are faced with one big question: should they go to university? Some students decide not to go. They might think that higher education is not necessary for them or that they have something more meaningful to do. Other students decide to go to university. Although these students all think that it is worth spending the next four years in classrooms, the reasons why they think so might be different.

- **Thesis statement:**
  Students go to university for a variety of reasons: academic interest, future career, or social life.

Body paragraph 1

- **Topic sentence:**
  First, many students attend university to study a particular subject in depth.

- **Supporting sentences:**
  University curriculums allow students to choose a major. This is a significant difference from high schools, which require students to take a wide range of classes regardless of their interests. Moreover, universities offer a number of specialized courses in one discipline, and these courses are taught by experts in the fields. Thus, for example, students who are interested in politics can major in political science and take courses about the political system, political philosophy, comparative politics, and other specific topics related to politics. In addition, universities have various research facilities that help students learn, such as libraries, laboratories, and computer rooms.

- **Concluding sentence:**
  Such curriculums, courses, faculty, and facilities enable students to pursue their academic goals in the field of their choice, and this is one of the reasons why they go to university.

Body paragraph 2

- **Topic sentence:**
  Another common reason for going to university is that a college education often leads to a better career in the future.

- **Supporting sentences:**
  In many countries, companies tend to look for university graduates to fill positions that have greater responsibility and higher pay, such as

managers and supervisors. Furthermore, for certain professions including doctors, lawyers, and school teachers, a university degree is a requirement. In addition, some universities provide students with opportunities to acquire practical skills that can be useful in the real world. For example, they offer courses in accounting, data processing, and foreign languages, as well as internship programs in which students can experience working in a company and learning business skills.

- **Concluding sentence:**
In short, some students attend university because a university degree and the practical skills they can acquire will bring them better employment opportunities in the future.

Body paragraph 3
- **Topic sentence:**
Finally, for some students, making friends and enjoying an active social life can be a sufficient reason to stay in school for another four years.

- **Supporting sentences:**
In universities, students have the chance to meet people who come from different places with diverse backgrounds. They might be in the same class with students who work while attending school, older people who returned to school after retirement, or students who come from other countries. In addition, universities have a variety of clubs and student organizations, such as sports teams, hobby groups, and social awareness groups. By joining them, students can spend time with others who have similar interests.

- **Concluding sentence:**
Thus, universities can be places to meet a diverse group of people and foster relationships, and these opportunities attract some students to higher education.

Concluding paragraph
- **Restatement of the thesis:**
In conclusion, students may have different reasons for going to university.

- **Summary of the body paragraphs:**
For many of them, the main reason is to explore the academic field they are interested in. However, some students attend university to gain an advantage in the job market in the future. Others go to university to meet people with different backgrounds and develop friendships.

- **Final thought:**
Regardless of the reason, it is important for students to remember why they are in university and do their best to achieve their goals.

3. a. (Topic) Reasons for going to university / (Opinion on the topic) Reasons for going to university vary.
   b. (1) academic interest, (2) future career, (3) social life

Exercise 2

p. 43

Answers will vary.

(Example answers)
1. University clubs can be classified into three types: sports, art, and academic.
2. Living in a dormitory is beneficial for university students because they can make friends, learn social skills, and save money.
3. Academic writing skills are important for university students because they help them complete course assignments successfully, obtain good grades, and gain an advantage in their future career.

Exercise 3

p. 45

Body paragraph 1
Problem:
The topic and the writer's opinion (reasons for going to university vary) are not included.

Body paragraph 2
Problem:
The controlling idea (future career) is not included.

Body paragraph 3
Problem:
The topic and the writer's opinion (reasons for going to university vary) are not included. The controlling idea (social life) is not expressed.

Exercise 4

p. 47

Answers can vary.

(Example answers)
1. First, by living in a dormitory, students can make friends.
2. Another benefit of living in a dormitory is that students can learn social skills.
3. Finally, dormitory life allows students to save money.

Exercise 5

p. 47

Answers will vary.

(Example answers)
1. Body paragraph 1: One of the common types of university clubs is sports clubs.
Body paragraph 2: Art clubs are another major type of university clubs.
Body paragraph 3: Finally, some university clubs are formed for academic purposes.

2. Body paragraph 1: First, academic writing skills are crucial in helping students complete university assignments successfully.
Body paragraph 2: Academic writing skills are also important because they can lead to good grades in university.
Body paragraph 3: The final reason for the importance of good academic writing skills is that they give students an advantage in their future career.

Exercise 6

p. 49

Body paragraph 1
3. Universities have various research facilities.

Body paragraph 2
2. Certain professions require a university degree.
3. Universities provide opportunities to acquire practical skills.

Body paragraph 3
1. Students can meet a diverse group of people
2. Students can join a club or student organization

Exercise 7

p. 50

Answers will vary.

(Example outline for topic 4, "Factors in choosing a university")

Topic: Factors in choosing a university

Thesis statement:
When students decide which university to attend, they take various factors into consideration, such as qualifications of professors, location, and cost.

Body paragraph 1
- **Topic sentence:**
  One factor that students consider when they choose their universities is if there are well-qualified professors to teach the major they want to study.

- **Supporting points:**
  1. Students want to study from experts in a field they are interested in.
  2. Some universities have famous professors in particular fields.
  3. Some students want to learn particular subjects from particular professors.

Body paragraph 2
- **Topic sentence:**
  Another important factor for students who are trying to decide which university to attend is whether it is in a suitable location or not.

- **Supporting points:**
  1. Students need to decide whether they should stay in their hometown or leave it when they go to university.
  2. The learning experience can be different depending on the school's location (urban or rural area).

3. Location affects the kinds of entertainment available on and off campus.

Body paragraph 3
- **Topic sentence:**
  Finally, many students think that it is important to examine the overall cost of education before they decide their universities.

- **Supporting points:**
  1. Tuition and living expenses – can afford to pay for four years?
  2. Tuition difference between public and private university
  3. Work and study to pay for the tuition?

UNIT 2 PART 2

Exercise 1

p. 53

Body paragraph 2
2. Doctors, lawyers, school teachers
3. Courses (accounting, data processing, foreign languages), internship programs

Body paragraph 3
1. Students who work while attending school, older students who returned to school after retirement, students from other countries
2. Sports teams, hobby groups, social awareness groups

Exercise 2

p. 54

Answers will vary.

(Example answers)

Body paragraph 1
1. Cooking, cleaning, doing the laundry
2. Lack of privacy, intrusive parents, having to share things with others, house rules (e.g., curfew)

Body paragraph 2
1. Have to follow rules (about leaving and returning, smoking and drinking, making noise, etc.), have to share rooms and facilities with other residents
2. Communicating with other people, making new friends, solving problems

Body paragraph 3
1. Can stay up late, sleep late, eat anything they like, smoke and drink, invite friends
2. Have to do all the housework, have to manage their budget, have to manage their health

Exercise 3

p. 58

1. d-a-c-e-b
2. e-b-f-d-a-c

Exercise 4

p. 59

Answers will vary.

(Example answers)

1. People today are suffering from a great deal of stress, and university students are no exception. Their lives change significantly from high school, and many students find it difficult to adjust for the first couple of months. One benefit of being a university student is that they have a lot of freedom because of the long breaks they have between semesters. However, considering the kinds of stress they may suffer during the semesters, such long breaks seem necessary to keep their mental balance. Common causes of stress among university students can be classified into three types: assignment deadlines, grades, and job hunting.

2. At some point during their high school lives, students are faced with an important question: should they go to university? The ones whose answer is "yes" to this question start gathering information about universities they may possibly apply to and compare the information. Students usually have a difficult time deciding which universities they should go to because of the unique characteristics each university possesses. However, when it comes to making the final decision, they tend to take similar factors into consideration. Majors, location, and tuition are three factors which many students consider when they choose a university.

Exercise 5

p. 61

Answers will vary.

(Example answers)

1. **Restatement of the thesis:**
   In conclusion, there are three common types of accommodation for university students.
   Restatement of the topic sentences:
   Students who already live nearby often decide to commute from their home. Those who live further away sometimes choose to move into a dormitory to live with other students. Others who do not like the restrictions of dormitories might choose to live on their own in an apartment.

2. **Restatement of the thesis:**
   To conclude, dormitory life provides numerous advantages for students.
   Restatement of the topic sentences:
   Making friends is easier in a dormitory than in other places on campus. In addition, life in a dormitory lets students develop their social skills. Moreover, students can save money by living in a dormitory.

3. **Restatement of the thesis:**
   To summarize, part-time employment brings several benefits to university students.
   Restatement of the topic sentences:
   For many, making money for personal use is a significant advantage of working part-time. Another equally important benefit is that students can develop skills that will be applicable when they get a real job. Finally, by working part-time, students obtain practical experience of different occupations.

Exercise 6

p. 65

Answers will vary.

(Example answers)

1. Because these three living situations have both advantages and disadvantages, students should consider their needs and desires carefully and choose the most suitable one.

2. Living in a dormitory offers students a rich and valuable personal experience.

3. Although the purpose of university is to study, it is clear why the benefits of a part-time job make it an attractive option for many students.

(Explanation)

1. This final thought is inappropriate because it uses *you* and is subjective in tone, so it should be rewritten from a third person's point of view by using words such as *students* and *their*.

2. This final thought is inappropriate because it uses the first person *I* and talks about personal experience which is irrelevant to what has been discussed in the essay. It should be rewritten from a third person's point of view to be more objective and to be relevant to the essay theme (living in a dormitory is beneficial).

3. This final thought is inappropriate because it tells students what they should do, which is not an intended purpose of this essay. It should be rewritten to be more relevant to the essay topic (advantages of working part-time for university students).

UNIT 2 PART 3

Exercise 1

p. 68

In the following, underlines indicate corrected parts.

Finally, living alone in an apartment is a choice among students who cannot commute to school from their homes but do not like the inconveniences of dormitory life. In this living situation, students can be free from their parents as well as the rules and restrictions of dormitory life. They can stay up as late as they want, eat whatever they like, and invite their friends to their place anytime. However, students are required to be independent and responsible in this living situation. As their parents do not watch them and take care of them, it is all up to the students to lead a healthy and orderly life. They have to do all the housework by themselves even when they are busy with their study. They have to manage their own budget so that they can save enough money for the rent, utilities, and other bills. In short, students who want freedom often choose to live by themselves in apartments, but they need to be mature enough to take care of themselves in this living situation.

Exercise 2

p. 70

1.
First Reading:
Content
1. No, all the information included in the essay is relevant to the thesis statement.

2. No, more specific details should be added, especially to body paragraph 3 (see **Comments** below).

3. Yes.

Organization
1. Yes.

2. The two sentences before the thesis statement are not enough for the building sentences. There should be more building sentences (see **Comments** below).

3. Yes/Yes.

4. Yes, but the topic sentences for body paragraphs 2 and 3 have other problems (see **Comments** below).

5. No, body paragraphs 1 and 3 can be developed more logically with more explanation and specific examples (see **Comments** below).

6. Yes.

7. No, a restatement of the topic sentences from the body paragraphs is missing in this essay.

8. Yes, but there are several mistakes with second-person pronouns (see **Problems with grammar and style** below).

Second reading:
1. Yes.

2. Mostly yes (see **Problems with grammar and style** below).

3. No, there are several mistakes (see **Problems with grammar and style** below).

4. Yes.

Comments:
Strengths:
- The thesis statement clearly states the writer's opinion and main ideas of the essay topic.
- The topic sentence of body paragraph 1 states the topic and the controlling idea clearly.
- The body paragraphs have relevant supporting points.
- The restatement of the thesis is good.

Weaknesses:
- There is not enough information in the building sentences in the introductory paragraph. The writer should add a few more sentences to link the first sentence to the thesis statement.
- The topic sentences of body paragraphs 2 and 3 do not include the writer's opinion on the topic. The writer should rewrite those sentences.
- Body paragraph 1 is confusing because the relationship between the ideas in each sentence is not signaled effectively.
- Body paragraph 3 is not developed well. The writer should include more details.
- There is no restatement of the topic sentences in the concluding paragraph.

2.
Problems with grammar and style:
- Sentence fragments:
  "For example, answering telephone, using cash register, and using computer" is not a grammatical sentence because it is missing a verb (see Unit 1 Part 3, page 30).

  "Because they need money for club activities, playing with friends, and buying favorite things" is a sentence fragment because it is a subordinating clause that is not attached to an independent clause (see Unit 1 Part 3, pages 22–25 and 30).

- Incorrect use of commas:
  In this sentence, *". . . one of the advantages of working part-time is, students can have extra money,"* the comma is used incorrectly to connect two clauses. The comma is not necessary in this sentence.

- Inappropriate transitional expression:
  Like this, is not an appropriate transitional expression because it is too colloquial.

- Use of *we* and *you*:
  Using second-person pronouns such as *we* and *you* in academic essays can degrade the tone of writing. The writer should use more appropriate pronouns such as *they* (see Unit 2 Part 3, page 67).

- Use of pronouns:
  Some of the nouns can be replaced with pronouns (see Unit 2 Part 3, pages 67–68).

- Use of contractions:
  Using contractions such as *don't* is not appropriate for academic essays because it is too colloquial (see Unit 1 Part 4, page 32).

Corrected draft:

Example of a corrected draft (<u>underlines</u> indicate corrected parts and <u>double underlines</u> indicate added parts):

Advantages of Working Part-Time for University Students

Nowadays, it is difficult to find university students who have never worked a part-time job. <u>While it is necessary to spend a lot of time studying at university, it is rare that students are so busy that they cannot fit in a part-time job.</u> <u>Many decide to take this option as it provides</u> many advantages for students. By working part-time, students can make extra money, develop various skills, and learn about different occupations.

First, by working part-time, students can have money that they can use freely. This is especially important for students who live alone because they have to pay for <u>an</u> apartment, electricity, water, food, and <u>other expenses</u> by themselves. Money from <u>a</u> part-time job <u>may not be</u> enough for paying all of these, but <u>they</u> can help their parents. Moreover, for students who <u>do not</u> live alone, it is important to have extra <u>money because</u> they need money for club activities, playing with friends, and buying <u>their</u> favorite things. In short, one of the advantages of working part-time <u>is that</u> students can have extra money.

<u>Another advantage of working part-time is that</u> students can learn various skills. <u>Most</u> part-time jobs require workers to communicate with people every day. For example, if <u>students work</u> in a restaurant, <u>they have</u> to greet customers and answer customers' questions politely. In addition, <u>they have</u> to communicate with <u>their</u> boss and coworkers to work smoothly. <u>Moreover,</u> some part-time jobs teach students practical skills <u>such as</u> answering <u>the</u> telephone, using <u>a</u> cash register, and using computer<u>s</u>. <u>In short</u>, students can learn skills that <u>they</u> cannot learn in university.

Finally, students can learn about different jobs <u>if they experience several part-time jobs while in university. University is often the last chance to enjoy freedom as students before working, so some students might not want to work at all. However, it is important to think about work while in university because students need to find jobs eventually. Working part-time is a perfect opportunity for them to decide their future career because they can learn about different jobs and think about what types of jobs are suited to them. In short, the experience of working part-time is useful when students try to find real jobs in the future</u>.

In conclusion, working part-time has many advantages for university students. <u>Part-time jobs give students some extra money. They also let students acquire skills that are not taught at school. Students who have worked part-time can also get clearer ideas about the jobs they want in the future</u>. It might be hard to work while going to school, but <u>students</u> should experience it at least once while <u>they</u> are in university.

UNIT 3 PART 1

Exercise 1

p. 74

(Answers)

1. a

2. b

(Explanation)

1. **a** is the best paraphrase because it expresses the original passage's meaning accurately in different words and grammar. **b** is not effective because its sentence structure and vocabulary are too close to the original passage (e.g., *"Because of the shortage of space, . . ."* is too similar to *"Due to the shortage of space, . . ."*). **c** is not appropriate because it does not keep all of the ideas in the original passage. Specifically, the idea that many universities in large cities do not have enough space for dormitories is not included in the paraphrase.

2. **b** is the best paraphrase because it expresses the original passage's meaning accurately in different words and grammar. **a** is not effective because it does not express the original passage's meaning accurately. The idea expressed in **a** is that the number of engineering schools is increasing, whereas the idea expressed in the original passage is that the number of women enrolling in engineering courses is increasing. **c** is inappropriate because its sentence structure and vocabulary are too close to the original (e.g., *". . . universities reported a consistent increase in the number of . . ."* is too close to *". . . universities have seen a steady increase in the number of . . ."*).

Exercise 2

p. 75

Answers will vary.

(Example answers)

1. The average citizen's diet is getting more international because imported food is available in many places.

2. Doctors say that the number of overweight teenagers has increased rapidly because young people sit for a long time using the internet or playing video games.

3. Having pets when they are young often makes people more relaxed as adults.

4. As well as removing the need for textbooks, tablet computers may radically change education.

5. A study in Australia showed the number of injuries suffered by athletes who warm up before exercising and those who don't to be the same.

Exercise 3

p. 77

(Answer)

a

(Explanation)

a is the best summary because it expresses the main ideas of the original text in much shorter form and in different words. **b** is not effective because it does not include all of the important ideas of the original text. The reason many people around the world use traditional medicine is not only because they cannot afford modern medicine, but also because it is effective and culturally significant. These ideas are missing in this summary. **c** is not effective because it is too long. It also contains structures that are too close to the original (e.g., *". . . inexpensive, easily accessible, and familiar natural ingredients"* is plagiarized from the original text).

Exercise 4

p. 79

Answers will vary.

(Example answers)

1. The Slow Food movement has gained support worldwide with its mission to protect traditional diets, promote safe and healthy food, and raise people's awareness of the food culture of their area.

2. Increased industrial impacts on the environment and the change to modern, global lifestyles over the last 40 years has contributed to a dramatic increase in allergies worldwide.

UNIT 3 PART 2

Exercise 1

p. 85

Answers for 1, 2, and 3 will vary depending on which in-text citation pattern is used. Citations are indicated in bold.

(Example answers)

1. **Rivers claims that** garbage left behind around Mount Everest by past climbers now poses a serious threat to the environment and a hazard to other climbers **(4)**.

2. **According to the United Nations Environment Programme**, major environmental problems caused by tourism include the depletion of natural resources, pollution, and various physical damages caused by construction and tourist activities **(5–6)**.

3. UCLA biologist Pat Farber said, "It is a failure of imagination that we humans cannot see value in animals beyond their use to us as food or entertainment" **(qtd. in Convertino 27)**.

4. Every year, an estimated 25 million vertebrate animals are used for the purpose of research, experiment and education in the U.S. **("Frequently Asked")**.

5. According to a United Nations report, approximately 25% of the mammals and 12% of the birds in the world might become extinct during the next few decades due to global warming **(qtd. in Schultz)**.

Exercise 2

p. 90

Corrections are indicated in bold.

1. It is reported that the value of the exotic pet industry has risen over 30% during the last five years to a massive $7.8 billion **(Rodriguez)**.

2. For example, according to the **Cascadia Fish and Wildlife Council**, many species of lizards, snakes, rodents, and turtles carry salmonella bacteria. (Explanation: Cascadia Fish and Wildlife Council should not be in italics).

3. **Nichols** states that when exotic animals kept as pets escape or are released by their owners, many survive and establish breeding populations in their new environment. These new foreign species often damage or destroy the native animal and plant species **(F2)**.

Exercise 3

p. 90

Works Cited

Convertino, John. "How We See Animals, How We See Ourselves." *Perspectives on Nature* May 2005: 27.

"Frequently Asked Questions about Animals in Research." *Animals in Research*. The Humane Society of the United States. Accessed 8 Dec. 2006 <http://www.hsus.org/animals_in_research.htm>.

Rivers, Jeremy. "A Mount Everest Makeover." *The Vancouver Globe* 2 Dec. 2005, late ed.: sec. 1:4.

Schultz, Roberta. "An Endangered Planet." *Ocean Tern News* 15 Feb. 2004. Accessed 5 Mar. 2007 <http://www.oceanternnews.com/environment/report/0529.htm>.

United Nations Environment Programme. *Environmental Impacts of Tourism*. Nairobi: United Nations Environment Programme, 2003.

UNIT 4 PART 1

<u>p. 94</u>

1. Components of each paragraph

<u>Introductory paragraph</u>

- **Building sentences:**
  Since humans first built boats and fished the seas, they have hunted whales. This practice remains culturally significant for many small communities around the world who hunt a few whales each year using traditional methods. In contrast, for other people, whaling has become a high-tech industry using sophisticated equipment to hunt and kill thousands of whales each year for profit. Although these whalers also cite cultural tradition to justify their annual hunts, commercial whaling is strongly opposed by an increasing number of people worldwide. Indeed, the practice of killing whales on an industrial scale is now internationally seen as morally wrong and economically unsound.

- **Thesis statement:**
  Therefore, commercial whaling should be banned because it causes excessive suffering to intelligent mammals, is no longer economically viable, and can be replaced by economically beneficial whale watching.

<u>Body Paragraph 1</u>
- **Topic sentence:**
  First, whaling should be banned because it is morally unacceptable to kill intelligent mammals brutally.

- **Supporting sentences:**
  Although the method of catching and killing whales has changed greatly over the years, it still remains cruel and ineffective. According to the World Society for the Protection of Animals, whales today are killed by explosive harpoons, which enter the whale near the head and explode inside its body. However, this method is far from effective as shown by the fact that only about 40% of the whales harpooned die immediately (2). In addition, these hunting methods go against modern society's acceptable standard of animal suffering. Benson found that "people surveyed around the world now correctly understand that whales are intelligent, social mammals, not fish, and if hunted, must receive instant, painless death" (88).

- **Concluding sentence:**
  Commercial whalers have shown that they cannot meet this international ethical standard, and thus this practice must stop.

<u>Body Paragraph 2</u>
- **Topic sentence:**
  Another reason why commercial whaling needs to cease is that it is no longer economically sustainable.

- **Supporting sentences:**
  First, whale meat is no longer a popular food even in countries that hunt whales commercially. Whale meat from past hunts is frozen and stored in warehouses, often for many years because consumer demand is so low ("Whaling"). This demonstrates a shift in modern eating habits. Eating whale is simply no longer considered desirable or necessary, and thus the shrinking market for it does not justify the amount of meat produced. This also results in governments subsidizing many whalers to keep them in business. With the meat supply far exceeding demand, Darby reports that the price of whale meat has dropped nearly 80% in some places (344). Many commercial whalers, therefore, rely on government money because the income earned from whaling is insufficient to make a living.

- **Concluding sentence:**
  In short, meat from commercial whaling no longer has a market, and whalers actually cost taxpayers considerable money by requiring government funds to cover their operating losses.

<u>Body Paragraph 3</u>
- **Topic sentence:**
  Finally, commercial whaling is no longer necessary because other business opportunities offer much better financial rewards.

- **Supporting sentences:**
  Today, ecotourism is a booming industry, and whale watching can be an important source of income for areas with large numbers of whales. For this reason, many developing countries, such as Argentina, Brazil and South Africa have banned whaling in their oceans and have promoted the development of whale watching industries (Holt 48). This has helped increase the number of visitors to these countries, and as a result, has brought profits to many local communities. For example, Valente reports that Puerto Madryn, a coastal city in Argentina, attracted only 17,000 whale watchers in 1991, but the number leaped to more than 100,000 by 2006.

- **Concluding sentence:**
  Thus, even if commercial hunting were banned, whaling countries could survive or even flourish more than before by promoting whale watching.

<u>Concluding paragraph</u>
- **Restated thesis:**
  In conclusion, as the evidence shows, whaling is cruel and economically unnecessary and therefore should be prohibited.

- **Summary of the body paragraphs:**
  The current method of killing whales causes intelligent mammals to suffer unnecessarily. Furthermore, because whale meat is no longer a significant part of people's diets, its price has fallen causing the industry to rely on public money. Finally, commercial whaling countries have no reason to continue hunting, as whale watching is an economically more preferable option.

- **Final thought:**
  Whaling has a long history and has played an important role in the past. However, social values and tastes have changed, and with change, some traditions adapt and survive while others cannot, and die. For commercial whaling, the latter seems inevitable and preferable.

2. a. The writer is against whaling.
   b. Whaling (1) causes excessive suffering to intelligent mammals, (2) is no longer economically viable, and (3) can be replaced by economically beneficial whale watching.

Exercise 2

p. 98

Answers will vary.

(Example answer for topic 1, "Are zoos necessary?")

For:
- People can learn about animals when they visit zoos
- People can learn to respect nature (animals' habitats)
- Zoos save endangered animals from extinction
- Zoos adopt exotic animals abandoned by their owners
- Zoos are ideal facilities for animal research

Against:
- Zoos are not educational – people cannot learn about animals in an unnatural environment
- Zoos give people an incorrect idea that humans are better than animals
- Zoos do not play an important role in conserving endangered species
- It is unethical to keep wild animals in cages
- Researching zoo animals does not provide useful information for wild animals

Writer's position:
Zoos are unnecessary.

Main ideas:
- It is unethical to keep animals in cages.
- People cannot learn accurate information about animals in zoos.
- Zoos are not successful in conserving endangered species.

Exercise 3

p. 99

Answers will vary.

(Example answers)

1. People should stop using animals for entertainment events because it makes animals suffer physically and mentally, these events can be replaced by other forms of entertainment, and seeing animals in shows encourages a disrespectful attitude towards other forms of life.

2. Owing exotic pets like parrots and monkeys should be banned because they are dangerous

wild animals, many of them are endangered species, and people cannot care for them properly.

3. Animal experiments should be banned because it is unethical to harm animals this way, alternative methods of experimentation are just as effective, and the benefits gained by animal testing are minor.

Exercise 4

p. 101

Answers will vary.

(Example answers)

1. First, people should stop using animals for entertainment because it makes animals suffer physically and mentally.
   Second, animal shows are unnecessary because they can be replaced by other forms of entertainment.
   The final reason why animals should not be used for people's entertainment is that it encourages a disrespectful attitude towards other forms of life.

2. First, exotic animals should not be allowed as pets because they are dangerous and wild.
   Another reason why owning exotic pets should be banned is that many of them are endangered species.
   Finally, because people cannot take proper care of exotic animals, they should not be allowed to keep them as pets.

3. The first reason why animal experiments should be banned is that it is unethical to harm animals in the name of testing.
   Second, animal experiments are no longer necessary because alternative methods are proven to be just as effective.
   Finally, the benefits gained by animal testing are minor, so people should stop using animals for experiments.

Exercise 5

p. 102

Body Paragraph 1

1. The method of whaling is cruel and ineffective.
2. Hunting methods go against modern society's acceptable standard of animal suffering.

Body Paragraph 2

1. Whale meat no longer has market value.
2. It is costing governments a lot of money to cover whalers' operating losses.

Body Paragraph 3

1. Whale watching can be an important source of income.
2. Whale watching has increased the number of tourists.

p. 104

Answers will vary.

(Example answer for "Are zoos necessary?")

Writer's position:
Zoos are unnecessary.

Main ideas:
It is unethical to keep animals in cages.

People cannot learn accurate information about animals in zoos.

Zoos are not successful in conserving endangered species.

OUTLINE

Topic: Are zoos necessary?

Thesis statement
Zoos are unnecessary because it is unethical to keep animals in cages, people cannot learn accurate information about animals in zoos, and zoos are not successful in conserving endangered species.

Body paragraph 1
- **Topic sentence:**
  To begin with, there is no need for zoos because confining animals in cages is an unethical practice.
- **Supporting points:**
  The amount of space animals in zoos get is not comparable to the space animals in the wild have. Animals in cages develop physical and psychological problems.

Body paragraph 2
- **Topic sentence:**
  Another reason why zoos are unnecessary is that it is impossible to learn accurate information about animals in these unnatural conditions.
- **Supporting points:**
  Most people go to zoos for fun; they do not go there for educational purposes.
  Animals in zoos behave differently from animals in the wild.

Body paragraph 3
- **Topic sentence:**
  The final reason that negates the necessity of zoos is that they are not playing an important role in saving endangered species from extinction.
- **Supporting points:**
  There are many endangered species in the world, but zoos can save only a few of them.
  Zoos try to help beautiful animals that can attract many visitors, but they are not so interested in helping other animals that are equally rare but not as beautiful or attractive.

UNIT 4 PART 2

Exercise 1

p. 108

1.
  Body paragraph 2:
  - Whale meat from past hunts is frozen and stored in warehouses, often for many years because consumer demand is so low ("Whaling").
  - With the meat supply far exceeding demand, Darby reports that the price of whale meat has dropped nearly 80% in some places (344).

  Body paragraph 3:
  - For this reason, many developing countries, such as Argentina, Brazil and South Africa have banned whaling in their oceans and have promoted the development of whale watching industries (Holt 48).
  - Valente reports that Puerto Madryn, a coastal city in Argentina, attracted only 17,000 whale watchers in 1991, but the number leaped to more than 100,000 by 2006.

2.
  Body paragraph 2:
  - The writer's idea: *"whale meat is no longer a popular food, even in countries that hunt whales commercially."*
  - The writer's idea: *". . . results in governments subsidizing many whalers to keep them in business."*

  Body paragraph 3:
  - The writer's idea: *". . . ecotourism is a booming industry, and whale watching can be an important source of income for areas with large numbers of whales."*
  - The writer's idea: *"This has helped increase the number of visitors to these countries, and as a result, has brought profits to many local communities."*

Exercise 2

p. 108

Argument 1:   b

Argument 2:   c

(Explanation)

For Argument 1, **b** supports the argument most effectively because it provides an example of a tiger wandering into a village and killing people. **a** does not support the argument effectively because "tigers rarely attack people" contradicts the argument "tigers sometimes attack people." **c** does not support the argument either because it talks about tiger attacks in rivers, but the argument is focused on tiger attacks in villages.

For Argument 2, **c** supports the argument most effectively because it gives a specific example of an Indian governmental program that tries to prevent contact between local villagers and tigers. **a** does not support the argument effectively because introducing people's reactions does not describe what the governmental programs actually do to prevent contact between local villagers and tigers. **b** does not support the argument effectively because talking about tigers' importance to Indian culture does not directly connect to the idea of keeping them away from villagers.

Exercise 3

p. 110

Answers will vary depending on whether students use quotation, paraphrase, or summary. Answers will also vary depending on which reporting verb students use.

(Example answers)

Statement 1:
(e) (Summary) Air pollution is a major problem in many national parks where motor vehicles are regular means of transportation for tourists. According to Taylor, harmful particles emitted from tourist cars contaminate the air in almost all national parks in California.

Statement 2:
(b) (Paraphrase) Tourism has posed serious threats to the rich marine life in coastal resorts around the world. Taylor claims that visiting divers and inconsiderate souvenir companies snap chunks of coral off reefs to take home, and cruise ships drop anchors and spill sewage onto reefs. All of these activities result in the death of coral, and 90 of the 109 countries with reefs report that the number of such incidents is increasing.

UNIT 4 PART 3

Exercise 1

p. 114

Answers will vary.

(Example answers)
1. <u>Some</u> zoos are creating more natural environments for their animals. / Zoos are <u>frequently</u> creating more natural environments for their animals.

2. People living in cities <u>often</u> keep their dogs in small apartments and do not give them enough exercise. / <u>Many</u> people living in cities keep their dogs in small apartments and do not give them enough exercise.

3. Horses are <u>usually</u> destroyed after breaking their leg during a race. / Horses are <u>likely to be</u> destroyed after breaking their leg during a race.

4. <u>Some of the</u> animals born in zoos cannot survive in the wild. / Animals born in zoos <u>may not be able to</u> survive in the wild.

5. When buying clothes that use fur, <u>few</u> people think how the animals were killed. / When buying clothes that use fur, people <u>rarely</u> think how the animals were killed.

6. Dogs and cats abandoned by their owners <u>are likely to</u> end up in animal shelters. / <u>Many</u> dogs and cats abandoned by their owners end up in animal shelters.

Exercise 2

p. 116

Step 1

First reading: content and organization

Content:
1. Yes.
2. Mostly yes (see **Comments** below).

Organization:
1. Yes.
2. The writer's position and the first two main arguments are expressed clearly, but the third main idea is missing.
3. The topic sentence for body paragraph 1 is good, but the topic sentences for body paragraphs 2 and 3 need improvement (see **Comments** below).
4. Mostly yes, but there is one missing element (see **Comments** below).
5. Yes, but it is not very effective (see **Comments** below).

Second reading: citation, grammar, and style

Citation:
1. Yes.
2. Yes, but there are a few mistakes (see **Problems with citation, grammar, and style** below).
3. Yes, but there are a few mistakes (see **Problems with citation, grammar, and style** below).
4. Yes, but there are several mistakes (see **Problems with citation, grammar, and style** below).

Grammar and style:
1. Mostly yes, but there is one mistake in the fourth paragraph.
2. Yes.
3. Yes.
4. No (see **Problems with citation, grammar, and style** below).
5. Yes.

Comments

Strengths:
- The writer's position is clear and consistent throughout the essay.
- Body paragraph 1 is developed well with a clear topic sentence, relevant supporting points, and details.

- Transitional expressions are effectively used.
- The concluding paragraph restates the thesis and summarizes the first two body paragraphs well.

Weaknesses:
- The thesis statement does not include all the main ideas (the main idea for body paragraph 3 is missing).
- Inappropriate citation in body paragraph 2 (*"Kenny says, when she wears fur, people usually compliment it and want to touch it"*). This is inappropriate because it is Kenny's personal remark and it does not support the writer's point (*"Natural fur looks and feels different from artificial fur"*) objectively and effectively.
- In body paragraph 3, the topic sentence refers to the essay writer (*"similar to my last point"*). This should be avoided.
- Concluding sentences are missing in body paragraphs 2 and 3.
- A summary of body paragraph 3 is missing in the concluding paragraph.
- The writer's final thought is not effective in the concluding paragraph. It is too simplistic and does not encourage readers to think about the topic after they finish reading the essay (see Unit 2 Part 2, page 64).

Step 2

Problems with citation, grammar, and style

Problems with citation (see Unit 3 Part 2, pages 83–90):
- Incorrect source names (two errors in body paragraph 1 and one error in body paragraph 3)
- Missing page number (one error in body paragraph 3)
- Three errors in the Works Cited list

Problems with grammar and style:
- Inappropriate vocabulary for academic writing (e.g., *Nowadays*, *like with seals*, *cute animals*)
- Use of first-person pronouns (see Unit 2 Part 3, page 67)

  This inappropriate use of pronouns disrupts the tone of an academic essay and should be avoided.
- Incorrect use of the coordinating conjunction *and* (body paragraph 3) (see Unit 1 Part 3, page 22–23)
- Overgeneralization (see Unit 3 Part 3, page 112)

  "For example, women wear fur coat they inherited from their grandmothers or great grandmothers" is an overgeneralization because not all women wear fur coats inherited from their grandmothers or great-grandmothers.

Corrected draft:
The following corrected draft only reflects the editing checklist, so some minor grammar

errors remain. In the following, underlines indicate corrected parts and double underlines indicate added parts.

Killing Animals for Fur

Recently, wearing animal fur is back in fashion. Many people wear coat and jacket bordered with fur. Fur is also used for shoes, hats, gloves, and scarves. People buy these items because they are fashionable and warm. Although some people are against it, humans should be allowed to kill animals for their fur because it is a natural thing for them and fur is special material that cannot be replaced by artificial material, and harvesting fur does not damage the animal population.

First, humans should be allowed to kill animals for their fur because it is a natural thing for them. Humans have always used animal fur as clothing. For example, according to Radcliffe, early humans wore fur tens of thousands of years ago (53). Even now, wearing fur is a part of daily life for some people. For instance, the Inuit people living in Arctic coastal areas wear boots and other clothing made from caribou or sealskin to protect themselves from cold weather (Thompson 25). Compared to the long history of fur clothes, the idea that wearing fur is wrong or killing animals is cruel is recent idea. In short, humans should be allowed to kill animals and use their fur because it is their natural way of life.

Second, killing animals for fur should not be regarded as problem because fur is very special material that cannot be replaced by artificial material. Natural fur looks and feels different from artificial fur. In addition, Kenny insists that the warmth real fur provides is not comparable to artificial fur because the basic constituents of each material are totally different. While natural fur is made of animals' hair and skin, fake fur is made of synthetic fabrics such as acrylic and polyester, which do not retain as much heat as real fur. In addition, natural fur is easier to produce and is more durable than artificial fur. Materials for fake fur such as acrylic and polyester require complicated production processes using chemicals, and the fur made out of such materials does not last for a long time. However, animal fur is easy to produce because it only requires catching and skinning animals. Moreover, it lasts longer, as evidence shows that some women wear fur coat they inherited from their grandmothers or great grandmothers. To sum up, using animals for their fur should not be stigmatized because artificial fur cannot become a substitute for real fur.

The final reason why humans should be allowed to kill animals for their fur is that it is a renewable natural product that does not negatively affect wildlife. In *Fur Over the Years*, Radcliffe says that fur comes from animals which are raised on farms specifically for that purpose. It is just like cows, pigs, chickens or salmon which are raised on farms only so people can eat them. Very few wild animals are used relative to the amount of fur produced. Even in cases where wild animals are used, such as seals, the number killed is closely controlled so the population of the seals is not negatively affected. In both cases, there is no bad effect on the animal populations, and the supply of fur is safely produced year after year. To summarize, because fur is largely produced on farms and carefully managed, it is a controlled and environmentally sustainable industry.

In conclusion, people should be allowed to kill animals for their fur. It is natural way of life that has continued for thousands of years. In addition, real fur is better quality than artificial fur. Moreover, animals being killed for their fur are the same as animals being killed for their meat. The idea that animals should not be slaughtered for their fur seems to come from people who do not know the reality of life. They need to recognize that producing and wearing fur is considered a natural part of life in many parts of the world.

Works Cited

Kenny, Mary. "Why I'm a Foxy Lady." *The Guardian Newspaper Online* 19 Jan. 2006. Accessed 2 Feb. 2007 <http://www.guardian.co.uk/animalrights/story/0,,1689814,00.html>.

Radcliffe, James. *Fur Over the Years*. Vancouver: Northern Pacific University Press, 2006.

Thompson, Joshua. "The Inuit: Traditions and Realities." *Modern Anthropology* Sep. 2004: 24–31.

For EU product safety concerns, contact us at Calle de José Abascal, 56–1°,
28003 Madrid, Spain or eugpsr@cambridge.org.

www.ingramcontent.com/pod-product-compliance
Ingram Content Group UK Ltd.
Pitfield, Milton Keynes, MK11 3LW, UK
UKHW050124160625
459711UK00022B/293